New Approaches to Economic Challenges

I0048092

The Financial System

Edited by
William Hynes, Patrick Love and Angela Stuart

》OECD

This work is published under the responsibility of the Secretary-General of the OECD. The opinions expressed and arguments employed herein do not necessarily reflect the official views of OECD member countries.

This document, as well as any data and map included herein, are without prejudice to the status of or sovereignty over any territory, to the delimitation of international frontiers and boundaries and to the name of any territory, city or area.

The statistical data for Israel are supplied by and under the responsibility of the relevant Israeli authorities. The use of such data by the OECD is without prejudice to the status of the Golan Heights, East Jerusalem and Israeli settlements in the West Bank under the terms of international law.

Note by Turkey
The information in this document with reference to "Cyprus" relates to the southern part of the Island. There is no single authority representing both Turkish and Greek Cypriot people on the Island. Turkey recognises the Turkish Republic of Northern Cyprus (TRNC). Until a lasting and equitable solution is found within the context of the United Nations, Turkey shall preserve its position concerning the "Cyprus issue".

Note by all the European Union Member States of the OECD and the European Union
The Republic of Cyprus is recognised by all members of the United Nations with the exception of Turkey. The information in this document relates to the area under the effective control of the Government of the Republic of Cyprus.

Please cite this publication as:
Hynes, W., P. Love and A. Stuart (eds.) (2020), *The Financial System*, New Approaches to Economic Challenges, OECD Publishing, Paris, *https://doi.org/10.1787/d45f979e-en*.

ISBN 978-92-64-32432-9 (print)
ISBN 978-92-64-59791-4 (pdf)

New Approaches to Economic Challenges
ISSN 2707-7926 (print)
ISSN 2707-7934 (online)

Preface

When I was appointed Secretary-General of the OECD in the summer of 2006, it was a pleasant, if unexciting, time to be an economist. The Great Moderation had already solved the problem of having continuous growth while keeping inflation under control. Deregulation had unleashed the creative energy of the financial system, ensuring that the economy would always have the funds it needed. And the science of economics had finally solved the problem of depressions, according to Nobel laureate Robert Lucas. A year later, that world fell apart. As I write these lines today, in the autumn of 2020, we are facing an even more serious situation, provoked by the Covid-19 virus. It is therefore important to identify significant parallels and differences with the great financial crisis (GFC), and to apply the policy lessons we have learned.

The first similarity is how crises arise. The traditional school of economic thought essentially sees the economy as a machine which almost always operates in a predictable, linear way. Occasionally, the machine gets knocked off balance, or out of equilibrium, and needs some resetting to get back on track. But the economy is not a machine, despite all our talk of "engines of growth" controlled by "policy levers". It is a complex adaptive system, with massive interdependencies among its parts and the potential for highly non-linear outcomes. In such systems, there is no equilibrium to return to. The crisis is not something that hits the system from outside. It is made possible and generated by the nature of the system itself.

Andy Haldane, Chief Economist of the Bank of England, discussed the similarities between financial crises and epidemics:

> *"Both events were manifestations of the behaviour under stress of a complex, adaptive network. Complex because these networks were a cat's-cradle of interconnections, financial and non-financial. Adaptive because behaviour in these networks was driven by interactions between optimising, but confused, agents. Seizures in the electricity grid, degradation of ecosystems, the spread of epidemics and the disintegration of the financial system – each is essentially a different branch of the same network family tree."*

Our approaches to economic analysis and policy anticipated neither the crisis, nor how it would cause an economic recession, and how the pain of that recession would provoke social and political crises in its wake. The results were rising inequalities, erosion of trust in governments and institutions, and growing populism which is influencing politics and economic policy. We created the New Approaches to Economic Challenges (NAEC) initiative to help policymakers design the analytical and practical tools they would need to address the kinds of interconnected challenges the 2008 crisis exemplified and foreshadowed.

An important lesson coming from NAEC is that the "system" in systemic is not one of the categories we traditionally used to identify and deal with crises – financial crisis, health crisis, political crisis... These are all subsystems of the greater system of systems composed of planet Earth and the human systems it supports. When NAEC calls for a systemic approach to avoiding collapse, that means understanding how an incident in one subsystem, even an initially insignificant one, can quickly be amplified and transmitted to become a threat to that system itself, and provoke cascading failures through other, interconnected systems. In 2007-2008, the spark was people defaulting on their debts in the US home loans market. In

2019-2020 it may have been a virus passing from bats, to pangolins, to humans in a Chinese wildlife market.

Cascading failures cause crises to lose their identities. We have to face not "just" a financial crisis or a pandemic. We have to deal with a crisis in which these are only two of the elements. Policymakers throughout history have said that their task is more difficult than before, but today there are good reasons to agree. In 2008, there was one immediate problem to solve – the imminent collapse of the banking system – and a limited number of actors involved, financial institutions and governments. Getting co-operation and immediate action in those circumstances is far easier than dealing with whole populations and whole economies.

There is however one major conclusion we can draw when comparing 2008 and today: policy decisions are central to producing the breeding ground for crises, to shaping how they will expand and evolve, and therefore to dealing with them. Governments decided to deregulate financial markets and decided on austerity as a response to the financial crisis that deregulation itself helped to bring about. In turn, austerity, and the drive for efficiency, left many health systems without the means to tackle Covid-19 effectively.

Both the 2008 and today's crises are teaching us another lesson: governments are the only system with the necessary fiscal and political 'firepower' to deal with the planetary emergencies we will continue to face throughout the 21st century. The OECD is ready to help our Member and partner countries, by sharing its expertise across the full range of policy domains that have to be incorporated into a systemic response to systemic threats of such magnitude.

Angel Gurría
Secretary-General
OECD

Foreword

The OECD launched its New Approaches to Economic Challenges (NAEC) initiative in 2012 to draw lessons from the policy and analytical failures of the 2008 crisis and to develop "A Strategic OECD Policy Agenda for Inclusive and Sustainable Growth". Since then, NAEC has catalysed a debate across the OECD and beyond on how to revise, update and improve policy thinking and action. The initiative promotes a systemic perspective on interconnected challenges with strategic partners, identifies the analytical and policy tools needed to understand them, and crafts the narratives best able to convey them to citizens and policymakers.

NAEC concluded that policymakers and economists underestimated the tensions that were building up before the crisis because traditional modelling and analytical approaches often failed to capture the complexity of the global economy and society as a whole. They underplayed the interconnectedness between and within economies, and in particular the relationship between financial markets and the real economy, as the financial system increasingly moved away from its original purpose of funding productive activities.

NAEC looked at how the economy itself was changing, how innovative economists were trying to understand these changes and reform the discipline, and what this meant both for how policies were designed and what the goal of those policies should be.

To move from analysis to policy solutions requires a new framework that would integrate the economy, and economics, with a range of other activities, insights and approaches to help tackle the planetary emergencies such as climate change and inequality that dominate the policy agenda. NAEC is co-ordinating projects on systems thinking, resilience to systemic threats, econophysics, neuroeconomics, integrative economics, and new economic thinking and acting generally.

The present volume presents NAEC's work on the financial system since the initiative was launched in 2012. William Hynes, Head of the NAEC Unit, was responsible for designing the conference and seminar programmes that provided the inputs to this collection of articles, and for developing and maintaining the network of contributing authors. Angela Stuart prepared the texts for publication and managed the publication process. Patrick Love edited the volume.

The support and encouragement of the co-chairs of the NAEC Group, Ambassador Irena Sodin of Slovenia and Ambassador Erdem Başçı of Turkey, contributed greatly to the success of NAEC work on the financial system.

Editorial

The OECD launched the New Approaches to Economic Challenges (NAEC) initiative in the wake of the 2008 financial crisis to understand the shortcomings of the analytical frameworks we had relied on and to establish the basis for a better way to produce policy advice. The obvious place to start was with economic models, but the problem was deeper than poor parameters and incomplete data. The models did not reflect the reality of the economy or of people's lives in that economy; and they did not anticipate how the pain of the recession would lead to social and political crises.

Why did so many highly competent people, using highly sophisticated techniques, not see the crisis that was coming? Why were we so comfortable with the results of our models, and the underlying assumptions? To put it simply, our analysis and understanding of financial markets and their impact on the real economy were not helpful in presenting the real level of risks we were confronting. In fact, the role of the financial system in traditional macroeconomic approaches rarely went beyond determining yield curves and stock prices.

In September 2018, NAEC convened experts on the financial system, including some who had played a role at the heart of the crisis, to discuss what we had learned from the experience of 2008. The group was diverse and the debate was lively, but there were repeated calls for macroeconomists to emphasise the complexities of the financial system in their models, rather than relying upon traditional methodological assumptions and modelling approaches. Adair Turner, Head of the UK Financial Services Authority (who writes on monetary finance in chapter 28), has gone so far as to say that "bad or rather over-simplistic and overconfident economics helped create the crisis".

The crisis and its aftermath exposed major flaws in the formation and assumptions of the standard macro-economic models – particularly concerns of computational irreducibility, emergence, non-ergodicity, and radical uncertainty, or Rick Bookstaber's (Chapter 5) "Four Horsemen of the Econopalypse". Jean-Claude Trichet (Chapter 15), found the traditional tools at his disposal of little use to address the serious economic policy challenges facing his institution in the midst of economic and financial meltdown.

Andy Haldane, Chief Economist of the Bank of England (Chapter 2) calls for the use of complexity theory to understand the overall architecture of public policy – how the various pieces of the policy jigsaw fit together as a whole in relation to the economic and financial systems. These systems can be characterised as a complex, adaptive "system of systems", whose architecture means that policies with varying degrees of magnification are necessary to understand and to moderate fluctuations. It also means that taking account of interactions between these layers is important when gauging risk. Bill White discusses some simple implications of complexity for policymakers (Chapter 11).

Unfortunately, financial interconnectedness, one of the apparent strengths of the global economy, makes risk assessment far more difficult to reliably execute than previously. Before 2008, market interconnectedness increased with the aid of policies encouraging the liberalisation of capital flows and the deregulation of derivative markets. After 2008, however, interconnectedness has been associated with the risk of financial contagion, where a toxic or failing financial institution impacts upon all others directly or indirectly. In mainstream economic science, such complexity and financial instability remains difficult to understand theoretically, let alone model quantitatively and inform international economic policy.

Fundamentally, we have limited ability to predict the threats which exploit financial and economic vulnerabilities and generate international economic recessions. We have limited capability to predict which economic threats may arise, how they will impact our financial and economic systems, or how to identify the correct steps needed to mitigate disruption or prevent it from occurring. However, there are indicators of potential sources of vulnerability, such as public and private debt. Governments, non-financial corporations, and households collectively owe USD 72 trillion more than they did in early 2008, and debt to GDP ratios have risen for many countries. Another indicator comes from financial market innovation, with high-speed algorithms trading the USD 3 trillion of passive exchange-traded products created since the crisis. Yet another source of vulnerability is the shadow-banking sector.

One of the most striking interventions at the 2018 NAEC conference came from John Llewellyn (Chapter 22), Chief Global Economist of Lehman Brothers in 2008. When asked if he saw any parallels between then and now, he replied that in both cases, experts, even within the major banks, were sounding warnings that decision-makers ignored. In the mid-2000s, those warnings focused upon the systemic fragility and growing weaknesses of the financial system due to the over-investment in highly risky and volatile assets. Today, Covid-19 has shown that there are multiple potential global systemic crises, each of which could disrupt many facets of daily life. Martin Wolf (Chapter 32), Michael Jacobs (Chapter 31) and Anat Admati (Chapter 30) highlight some of the dangers ahead with regard to financial leverage and debt. Mathilde Mesnard and Robert Patalano (Chapter 33) discuss new vulnerabilities.

What can policymakers do about this grim reality?

First, accept that new crises will occur and they will not be limited to one domain – a health emergency can quickly become a financial and economic crisis, as happened with Covid-19. Whatever their initial label, all crises have similar features that should be considered when designing policy approaches to recovery and adaptation in the aftermath of a systemic upheaval. The tensions already exist, and the cascading impacts of a crisis that spreads from one domain to others will impose significant strains on most socio-political systems, and, as we have seen, force governments to make difficult choices.

Second, policymakers will need new tools to understand complexity and to manage rising levels of risk under conditions of uncertainty in an interconnected, non-linear, systemic world. Economic systems should be modelled and managed as complex adaptive systems (See Andrew Lo in Chapter 4 on adaptive markets).

Finally, we need to shift from risk-based to resilience-based approaches to model and govern the financial system and other systems. Resilience-based approaches cannot predict the cause of the next global recession, but they can limit the scope of any potential contagion, and improve the pace and scale of economic recovery. Resilience approaches focus on the ability of a system to absorb, recover from, and adapt to a wide array of shocks to help individuals, communities, and larger groupings not just deal with adversity, but adapt in a positive way to change and take advantage of the opportunities it offers. While the financial regulatory and supervisory framework has been substantially strengthened since 2008, there is still scope to integrate resilience more effectively in our policies and monitoring tools.

Juan Yermo
Chief of Staff, OECD

Table of contents

Executive Summary

The 2008 financial crisis revealed failings in the way economists treated the financial system in relation to the real economy and the way regulators dealt with it. The crisis taught us three lessons: finance is central to macroeconomic outcomes; multiple equilibria can be all-important under stressful conditions; and the political economy of policy matters.

The crisis arose from the interaction of several characteristics. First, the extreme sophistication of financial instruments and the development of securitisation, the generalisation of derivative markets, the rapid growth of shadow banking, and the emergence of highly-leveraged institutions. Second, increased interconnectedness between all financial and non-financial institutions, enabled and encouraged by the advance of information technologies, giving rise to new, untested properties of global finance. At the same time, a sentiment of excessive tranquillity and confidence both in the public and private sectors due to sustained growth with low inflation. Third, belief in a "Great Moderation", a permanent reduction in the volatility of business cycle fluctuations thanks to institutional and structural change. Fourth, consensus in the international community on the efficiency of markets in almost all circumstances, justifying large deregulation. The belief that the financial system could never be far away from a single optimal equilibrium. Fifth, generalised excess leverage was totally neglected by the international community. The explosion of leverage was boosted by the 'shadow banking' world of hedge funds, private equity firms, and other unregulated financial companies. When asset values turned, confidence and trust collapsed and leverage became destructive. Incentive structures encouraged traders to make unwarrantedly risky bets, but all traders have individual risk limits and banks' managements set those limits.

The possibility of financial developments as drivers of economic performance was also largely ignored. In macroeconomic models, the role of the financial system was often reduced to the determination of a yield curve and stock prices. Fluctuations were seen as regular random shocks. In reality, financial crises are characterised by non-linearities and positive feedback whereby shocks are strongly amplified rather than dampened as they propagate. Financial markets, and economic behaviour generally, are a product of human evolution, and the basic principles of mutation, competition, and natural selection apply to the banking industry as much as to natural ecosystems. The key to these laws is adaptive behaviour in shifting environments.

One shift is that rather than returning to the status quo when the shock ends, financial crises are followed by long periods of depressed output. Another non-linearity comes from the interaction between public debt and the banking system, so-called "doom loops". Higher public debt leads to worries about public debt restructuring, decreasing the value of the bonds held by financial institutions, leading in turn to a decrease in their capital, worries about their health, and the expectation that the state may have to bail them out and be itself in trouble as a result. A boom-bust process driven by private credit also fuels crises: excessive private debt and credit before crisis, negative credit during it (the annual change in private debt being negative rather than positive).

Financial networks therefore are not random, and are likely to have network properties that manifest a statistical signature of complex systems, namely, a top tier multi-hub of few agents who are highly connected among themselves and to other nodes that show few if any connections to others in the periphery. The clustered structure of a network implies short path lengths between a node and any other node in the system. This is efficient in terms of liquidity and informational flows in good times, but worsens fragility in bad times when so-called hub banks ('super-spreaders') fail or suffer illiquidity.

The analogy with policies designed to suppress natural disasters should be kept in mind, especially the trade-off between efficiency and resilience. Extinguishing every small fire in a forest may seem like a useful precaution, but it allows undergrowth to proliferate, adding potential fuel to future fires, just as dampening volatility in financial markets encourages risk-taking and increases the chances of a crisis.

Agent-based models (ABM) are a better way to understand the financial system than more traditional approaches. They use a dynamic system of interacting, autonomous agents to allow macroscopic behaviour to emerge from microscopic rules. Likewise, the agent-based approach recognises that individuals interact and thereby change the environment, leading to the next interaction. ABM operate without a representative consumer or investor who is always right. They allow for construction of a narrative, unique to the particular circumstances in the real world, in which the system may be derailed. Narratives are not just a way describing and seeking to understand what has happened. Stories that "go viral" evolve to actually affect outcomes, including crises, depressions, and recessions. The narrative basis of economic phenomena might be hard to see since narratives are not easy to measure, but by incorporating an understanding of popular narratives into their explanations, economists will become more sensitive to such influences and may produce better forecasts.

As models become more realistic, analytics often has to give way to numerical simulations. This is well-accepted in physics, but many economists are still reluctant to recognise that numerical investigation of a model, although very far from theorem proving, is a valid way to do science. Numerical experiments allow one to quickly qualify an agent-based model (ABM) as potentially realistic or completely off the mark. What makes this expeditious diagnosis possible is the fact that for large systems details do not matter much – only a few microscopic features end up surviving at the macro scale.

Before the crisis, both monetary and prudential policies eased gradually over three decades. Afterwards, monetary easing continued but was accompanied with a justifiable degree of tightening in prudential policies. The big question was whether monetary policy could be normalised and what that 'new normal' would look like, in particular, if negative interest rates become a permanent feature of the new normal. The Covid-19 crisis suggests that this is the wrong question to ask. Underlying it is an implicit assumption that it is possible to get back to some theoretically "normal" state that was disrupted. The experiences of 2008 and 2020 suggest that constant flux and potential crises are the new normal, and the financial system should not be seen in isolation from the broader socio-economic and environmental system it is part of.

1 Theory and Models of the Financial System

This section reviews the theory and models of the financial system and examines what causes financial crises. It discusses what history teaches us about crises, and argues that the economic crisis that started in 2008 provoked a crisis in economic science. The section outlines three lessons and three trilemmas that characterise economics after the 2008 crisis. It describes the Adaptive Markets Hypothesis and considers how agent-based models and approaches adapted from physics could be used to better understand the financial system. Financial network analysis and narrative economics are suggested as ways to analyse and understand how actors at different scales make economic decisions and how they interact.

1. Economists need to abandon their comfort zones to deal with Covid-19

Rana Foroohar
© *The Financial Times, 3 May 2020*

I am always surprised by how linear most economic thinking is. Economists take a stand on a particular issue - free trade is either working or it isn't; regulation is needed or is not - and then refuse to leave their silos, even when the real world turns out again to be a messy and complex place.

The profession, sadly, is not as variegated - yet. It's true that since the 2008 financial crisis we have moved from the neoclassical notion that the invisible hand is always right to a world in which economists also consider human bias, politics and institutional realism when crafting their models. Yet there's still a general presumption that countries, companies, markets and individuals will eventually reset to "normal".

Linear systems and baseline reversion to equilibrium is generally assumed. And efficiency rather than resiliency is encouraged. It was also the mainstream economics taught in universities and business schools over the past 40 years. It supported the just-in-time business culture in which redundancy in supply chains was considered a waste of time and money and the free flow of capital across borders to create more economic growth was always a good thing, despite any inequality and financial fragility they might create.

Covid-19 is ripping the scales from our eyes on such assumptions. It is also driving home an important message that policymakers need to heed. If the economics profession is going to help solve the world's biggest problems - from pandemics and climate change to deglobalisation and inequality - economists must stop tweaking the edges of their models and think outside the box.

Much of the debate about how to reopen countries and cities in the wake of coronavirus has, for example, been incremental: take away X amount of social distancing, and get X amount of growth, and so on. It is as if there are some easy- to-define numerical trade-offs between the two.

"These types of phenomenon don't work like that," says William Hynes, the head of the OECD's New Approaches to Economic Challenges unit, set up in the wake of the financial crisis to study how to do better policymaking within complex systems. "Pandemics aren't linear — they are exponential. When things get knocked off track, they don't always come back to a steady state. We're talking about complex systems." The same goes for the environment, populism or the financial system and, of course, the global economy.

One of the most outside-the-box economic thinkers I know, Bank of England chief economist Andy Haldane, once likened Sars to the Lehman Brothers failure.

Imagining how Covid-19 will play out - and how the corporate debt crisis or unprecedented monetary and fiscal policies may unfold - will require more creative and complex thinking than we see in most mainstream economics today. Efficiency is homogenous. Profit maximisation and shareholder "value" are clear and relatively simple to understand concepts, even if they create myriad hidden risks.

"Resiliency, on the other hand, is heterodox," as former World Trade Organization director-general Pascal Lamy put it last week at a conference on building more shockproof global systems. Building resiliency in economic systems is harder than promoting efficiency, but ultimately it may be more rewarding.

Economists who want to help solve the world's problems should embrace variety and complexity. The economics profession, despite some strides towards diversity, is still nearly as black and white in its thinking as are the politicians that the profession advises (I say this as someone who talks regularly to both groups and constantly has to explain how I can be both a Democrat and care about the ramifications of public debt). Economists should not only talk to more peers on the other side of the ideological spectrum, but to other experts too - biologists, environmentalists, defence experts, security analysts, engineers - and even real people.

Sources

New Approaches to Economic Challenges (NAEC) https://www.oecd.org/naec/

OECD/NAEC-OMI conference: Shock-proof: Building Resilient Systems in the 21st Century
https://www.oecd.org/naec/events/systemic-linkages/building-resilient-systems-in-21st-century.htm

2. From economic crisis to crisis in economics

Andrew G. Haldane

It would be easy to become very depressed at the state of economics in the current environment. Many experts, including economics experts, are simply being ignored. But the economic challenges facing us could not be greater: slowing growth, slowing productivity, increased protectionism, the retreat of globalisation, high and rising levels of inequality. These are deep and diverse problems facing our societies and we will need deep and diverse frameworks to help understand them and to set policy in response to them. In the pre-crisis environment when things were relatively stable and stationary, our existing frameworks in macroeconomics did a pretty good job of making sense of things.

But the world these days is characterised by features such as discontinuities, tipping points, multiple equilibria, and radical uncertainty. So if we are to make economics interesting and the response to the challenges adequate, we need new frameworks that can capture the complexities of modern societies.

We are seeing increased interest in using complexity theory to make sense of the dynamics of economic and financial systems. For example, epidemiological models have been used to understand and calibrate regulatory capital standards for the largest, most interconnected banks, the so-called "super-spreaders". Less attention has been placed on using complexity theory to understand the overall architecture of public policy – how the various pieces of the policy jigsaw fit together as a whole in relation to modern economic and financial systems. These systems can be characterised as a complex, adaptive "system of systems", a nested set of sub-systems, each one itself a complex web. The architecture of a complex system of systems means that policies with varying degrees of magnification are necessary to understand and to moderate fluctuations. It also means that taking account of interactions between these layers is important when gauging risk.

Although there is no generally-accepted definition of complexity, that proposed by Herbert Simon in The Architecture of Complexity - "one made up of a large number of parts that interact in a non-simple way" - captures well its everyday essence. The whole behaves very differently than the sum of its parts. The properties of complex systems typically give rise to irregular, and often highly non-normal, statistical distributions for these systems over time. This manifests itself as much fatter tails than a normal distribution would suggest. In other words, system-wide interactions and feedbacks generate a much higher probability of catastrophic events than Gaussian distributions would imply.

For evolutionary reasons of survival of the fittest, Simon posited that "decomposable" networks were more resilient and hence more likely to proliferate. By decomposable networks, he meant organisational structures which could be partitioned such that the resilience of the system as a whole did not rely on any one sub-element. This may be a reasonable long-run description of some real-world complex systems, but less suitable as a description of the evolution of socio-economic systems. The efficiency of many of today's networks relies on their hyper-connectivity. There are, in the language of economics, significantly increasing returns to scale and scope in a network industry. Think of the benefits of global supply chains and global interbank networks for trade and financial risk-sharing. This provides a powerful secular incentive for non-decomposable socio-economic systems.

Moreover, if these hyper-connected networks do face systemic threat, they are often able to adapt in ways which avoid extinction. For example, the risk of social, economic or financial disorder will typically lead to an adaptation of policies to prevent systemic collapse. These adaptive policy responses may preserve otherwise-fragile socio-economic topologies. They may even further encourage the growth of connectivity and complexity of these networks. Policies to support "super-spreader" banks in a crisis for instance may encourage them to become larger and more complex. The combination of network economies and policy responses to failure means socio-economic systems may be less Darwinian, and hence decomposable, than natural and biological systems.

What public policy implications follow from this complex system of systems perspective? First, it underscores the importance of accurate data and timely mapping of each layer in the system. This is especially important when these layers are themselves complex. Granular data is needed to capture the interactions within and between these complex sub-systems.

Second, modelling of each of these layers, and their interaction with other layers, is likely to be important, both for understanding system risks and dynamics and for calibrating potential policy responses to them.

Third, in controlling these risks, something akin to the Tinbergen Rule is likely to apply: there is likely to be a need for at least as many policy instruments as there are complex sub-components of a system of systems if risk is to be monitored and managed effectively. Put differently, an under-identified complex system of systems is likely to result in a loss of control, both system-wide and for each of the layers.

In the meantime, there is a crisis in economics. For some, it is a threat. For others it is an opportunity to make a great leap forward, as Keynes did in the 1930s. But seizing this opportunity requires first a re-examination of the contours of economics and an exploration of some new pathways. Second, it is important to look at economic systems through a cross-disciplinary lens. Drawing on insights from a range of disciplines, natural as well as social sciences, can provide a different perspective on individual behaviour and system-wide dynamics.

The NAEC initiative does so, and the OECD's willingness to consider a complexity approach puts the Organisation at the forefront of bringing economic analysis policy-making into the 21st century.

Sources

From economic crisis to crisis in economics, OECD Insights
http://oecdinsights.org/2017/01/11/from-economic-crisis-to-crisis-in-economics/

NAEC Roundtable, OECD, 14 December 2016, http://video.oecd.org/players/dImpBtVZ-zLampSRtlFiNFxaLN1Z7FtwkYN18--Gm2b2LSng85YLWggTcxKx2OqA9sgDoGK2bb5FCgme1SLoCg

"The dappled world" GLS Shackle Biennial Memorial Lecture, 10 November 2016
https://www.bankofengland.co.uk/-/media/boe/files/speech/2016/the-dappled-world.pdf

"On microscopes and telescopes", Lorentz Centre, Leiden, Workshop on socio-economic complexity, 27 March 2015 https://www.bankofengland.co.uk/speech/2015/on-microscopes-and-telescopes

3. What does history teach us about crises?

Michael Bordo

Economic development and growth in the past two centuries have been facilitated by stabilising monetary and financial regimes, in large part thanks to central banks developing policy tools to provide both macroeconomic and financial stability. Macroeconomic stability comprises price level stability (today low inflation); limited volatility in the real economy (smoothing the business cycle) and financial stability. Traditionally, financial stability meant preventing and managing financial crises but recently it has come to mean heading off systemic risk (imbalances) and especially credit-driven asset price booms and busts which can trigger financial crises. Since the Global Financial Crisis (GFC) of 2008, central banks have focused increasingly on their financial stability mandate and especially the link between credit-driven asset price booms and busts which many view as the key cause of financial crises.

The consensus among economists and policy makers is that credit driven asset price booms are the key cause of serious financial crises. The existence of such a link can be tested first by surveying the co-evolution of monetary policy and financial stability and the historical evidence on the incidence, costs and determinants of financial crises; then looking at empirical historical evidence on the relationships between credit booms, asset price booms and serious financial crises. This will help answer the question of whether the two serious financial crises which were linked to credit-driven asset price booms and busts, the 1929-33 "Great Contraction" and the GFC, should be grounds for permanent changes in the monetary and financial environment.

To provide some empirical perspective, I examined the evidence for a sample of 15 advanced countries from 1880 to the present to see if credit booms associated with banking crises peak slightly before or are coincident with banking crises; if equity boom busts and housing price boom busts associated with banking crises occur shortly before or coincident with serious banking crises; and to determine the relationship between these types of events and banking crises associated with severe recessions.

The results suggest that credit boom induced big crises like the Great Contraction or the GFC are very rare - about once in every 50 years - and that credit booms are not very closely connected to asset price booms. Credit driven asset price booms were important in a few big crises before World War II but not the majority. Financial instability has though returned with the return of financial globalisation since the collapse of Bretton Woods and the liberalisation of domestic financial sectors. Since the 1970s major financial innovation has allowed banks to fund themselves in the financial markets and not have to rely on deposits. This has allowed bank credit to grow faster than the money supply, has increased leverage, and may have been a key factor triggering asset price booms and possible financial crises since the 1980s.

 In addition, financial innovation, made possible by the growth of financial theory and financial innovation, has led to the growth of non-bank financial intermediaries (shadow banks) which are outside the traditional supervisory and regulatory networks. These innovations both in the traditional banking sector and the shadow banking sector have increased both leverage and liquidity in the financial system. This has created a new source of systemic risk which can increase financial instability.

Moreover, output losses in the period since 1997 are much larger than in the pre-1914 period despite today's greater reliance on lender of last resort policies and other policies designed to remedy the market failures associated with financial shocks. This may be explained by the fact that in recent years deposit insurance and the financial sector safety net created guarantees of the financial system which converted banking panics into fiscally resolved financial crises which became increasingly more expensive to resolve. The stakes associated with financial crises have therefore been higher, reinforcing the imperative for monetary authorities to prevent them.

The means to do so should however be considered carefully before advocating radical reform. After the Great Contraction the world's monetary authorities believed that a sea change in monetary policy and financial stability policy was called for, and repressed both the domestic and international financial system for 40 years. That strategy led to unintended consequences driven by the dynamics of financial innovation and may in turn have sown the seeds for the GFC 80 years later. An obsession with financial stability (and the increased use of the tools of macroprudential policy and "leaning against the wind" by using monetary policy tools to head off imbalances) raises the risk of repeating the mistakes of the 1930s and creating a new regime of financial repression which will also have unintended consequences.

The analogy with policies designed to suppress natural disasters should be kept in mind, especially the trade-off between efficiency and resilience. Extinguishing every small fire in a forest may seem like a useful precaution, but it allows undergrowth to proliferate, adding potential fuel to future fires, just as dampening volatility in financial markets encourages risk-taking and increases the chances of a crisis.

A key lesson from the historical record through the Great Moderation period is that if four key principles are followed a stable monetary policy regime can be compatible with financial stability: price stability (credibility for low inflation); real macro stability (via e.g. flexible inflation targeting); a credible rules-based lender of last resort, and sound financial supervision and regulation and banking structure. Canada, which followed these principles, avoided banking crises altogether.

The GFC and the Great Recession were contained by effective monetary and fiscal policies and an unorthodox extension of the lender of last resort by the Fed and other authorities who had learned the lessons of the 1930s. However, like the 1930s, the GFC was blamed on the banks and the financial system and this has led to the creation of a new regime of financial regulation and the elevation of the financial stability mandate to primary importance. In addition to financial repression, the adoption of many of the tools of macroprudential regulation that have been proposed may recreate the problems with the use of these tools in the past.

Many of these macroprudential policies were actually credit or fiscal policies which greatly involved the monetary authorities in inefficiently picking winners and losers and influencing the allocation of resources. They also harmed central bank independence because these policies strayed from their mandates and opened them up to scrutiny and criticism by the legislature. An enhanced financial stability strategy may put out some small fires in the coming years, but precipitate an even bigger crisis than 2008 a few decades from now.

A knowledge of history matters. Basing important regime-changing decisions on the last crisis ignores the heterogeneity of crises. History teaches us the importance of relearning the details of the events of the past which often contain important and long forgotten clues to aid in our understanding of a current crisis.

Sources

NAEC seminar "The Great Financial Crisis and the Recovery", OECD, 4 September 2018
http://www.oecd.org/naec/events/great-financial-crisis-and-recovery.htm

"An historical perspective on the quest for financial stability and the monetary policy regime" NBER Working Paper 24154, December 2017 http://www.nber.org/papers/w24154

4. The Adaptive Markets hypothesis

Andrew Lo

Economic behaviour and financial markets are a product of human evolution, and as such are shaped by biological laws. The basic principles of mutation, competition, and natural selection apply to the banking industry as much as to natural ecosystems. The key to these laws is adaptive behaviour in shifting environments. To understand the complexity of human behaviour, we need to understand the different environments that have shaped it over time and across circumstances. We need to understand how the financial system functions and sometimes fails under these different conditions. We have assumed rational economic behaviour for so long that we've forgotten about other aspects of human behaviour.

Neuroscience and evolutionary biology confirm that rational expectations and the Efficient Markets Hypothesis (EMH) capture only some of the full range of human behaviour. That is not to say we should discard EMH altogether. It takes a theory to beat a theory, and the behavioural finance literature has yet to offer a clear alternative that does better. Psychology, neuroscience, evolutionary biology, and artificial intelligence can all help us to understand market behaviour, but none of them offers a complete solution. We need a new narrative for how markets work, and now have enough pieces of the puzzle to start putting it all together.

We begin by acknowledging that market inefficiencies exist. These inefficiencies and the behavioural biases that create them are important clues into how the brain makes financial decisions. We've seen how biofeedback measurements can be used to study behaviour, and can use imaging techniques to watch how the human brain functions in real time as we make decisions. However, neuroeconomics is only one layer. For example, neuroscience can tell us why people with dopamine dysregulation syndrome become addicted to gambling, but it doesn't explain anything about the larger picture of financial decision making. To the sceptic, the peculiar behaviours described in these neuroscientific case studies are really just "bugs" in the basic program of economic rationality, the exceptions that prove the rule.

In fact, we have to turn the standard economic view of human rationality on its head. We aren't rational actors with a few quirks in our behaviour. Our brains are collections of quirks. Working together, under certain conditions, these quirks often produce behaviour that an economist would call "rational." But under other conditions, they produce behaviours that an economist would consider wildly irrational. These quirks are the products of brain structures whose main purpose isn't economic rationality, but survival.

Our neuroanatomy has been shaped by the long process of evolution, changing only slowly over millions of generations. Our behaviours are shaped by our brains. Some of our behaviours are evolutionarily old and very powerful. The raw forces of natural selection, reproductive success or failure— in other words, life or death— have engraved those behaviours into our very DNA. Natural selection gave us abstract thought, language, and the memory-prediction framework. These adaptations give us the power to change our behaviour within a single lifespan, in response to immediate environmental challenges and the anticipation of new challenges. Natural selection also gave us heuristics, cognitive shortcuts, behavioural biases, and other conscious and unconscious rules of thumb— the adaptations that we make at the speed of thought. Natural selection isn't interested in exact solutions and optimal behaviour, features of Homo economicus. Natural selection only cares about differential reproduction and elimination, in other words, life or death. Our behavioural adaptations reflect this cold logic. However, evolution at the speed of thought is far more efficient and powerful than evolution at the speed of biological reproduction, which unfolds one generation at a time. Evolution at the speed of thought allows us to adapt our brain functions across time and under myriad circumstances to generate behaviours that have greatly improved our chances for survival.

This is the core of the Adaptive Markets Hypothesis, whose basic idea can be summarised in five key principles:

1. We are neither always rational nor irrational, but we are biological entities whose features and behaviours are shaped by the forces of evolution.

2. We display behavioural biases and make apparently suboptimal decisions, but we can learn from past experience and revise our heuristics in response to negative feedback.

3. We have the capacity for abstract thinking, specifically forward-looking what- if analysis; predictions about the future based on experience; and preparation for changes in our environment. This is evolution at the speed of thought, which is different from but related to biological evolution.

4. Financial market dynamics are driven by our interactions as we behave, learn, and adapt to each other, and to the social, cultural, political, economic, and natural environments in which we live.

5. Survival is the ultimate force driving competition, innovation, and adaptation.

Under the Adaptive Markets Hypothesis, individuals never know for sure whether their current heuristic is "good enough." They make choices based on their experience and their best guess as to what might be optimal. They learn by receiving positive or negative reinforcement from the outcomes. As a result of this feedback, individuals will develop new heuristics and mental rules of thumb to help them solve their various economic challenges. As long as those challenges remain stable over time, their heuristics will eventually adapt to yield approximately optimal solutions to those challenges.

The Adaptive Markets Hypothesis can easily explain economic behaviour that is only approximately rational, or that misses rationality narrowly. But it can also explain economic behaviour that looks completely irrational, as when the environment changes and the heuristics of the old environment might not be suited to the new one. Or when individuals receive no reinforcement from their environment, and don't learn. Likewise, inappropriate reinforcement will teach individuals suboptimal behaviour. And if the environment is constantly shifting, individuals may never reach an optimal heuristic. This, too, will look "irrational."

The Adaptive Markets Hypothesis recognises that suboptimal behaviour is going to happen when we take heuristics out of the environmental context for which they emerged. Even when an economic behaviour appears extremely irrational, it may still have an adaptive explanation. Such behaviour isn't "irrational," but "maladaptive." Our behaviour adapts to new environments both in the short term as well as across evolutionary time, and not always in financially beneficial ways. Financial behaviour that may seem irrational now is behaviour that has not had sufficient time to adapt to the context. Economic expansions and contractions are the consequences of individuals and institutions adapting to changing financial environments, and bubbles and crashes are the result when the change occurs too quickly.

Sources

NAEC seminar "New approaches to financial markets", OECD, 20 October 2017, https://youtu.be/MW6zqaKP-dU

Adaptive Markets: Financial Evolution at the Speed of Thought, Andrew W. Lo, Princeton University Press, 2019

5. Agent-based models

Richard Bookstaber

Traditional economics cannot address well four characteristics of human experience that manifest themselves in crises. The first of these "Four Horsemen of the Econopalypse" is computational irreducibility. You may be able to reduce the behaviour of a simple system to a mathematical description that provides a shortcut to predicting its future behaviour, the way a map shows that following a road gets you to a town without having to physically travel the road first. Unfortunately, for many systems you only know what is going to happen by faithfully reproducing the path the system takes to its end point, through simulation and observation, with no chance of getting to the final state before the system itself. It's a bit like the map Borges describes in *On Rigor in Science*, where "the Map of the Empire had the size of the Empire itself and coincided with it point by point". Not being able to reduce the economy to a computation means you can't predict it using analytical methods, but economics requires that you can.

The second characteristic property is emergence. Emergent phenomena occur when the overall effect of individuals' actions is qualitatively different from what each of the individuals are doing. You cannot anticipate the outcome for the whole system on the basis of the actions of its individual members because the large system will show properties its individual members do not have. For example, some people pushing others in a crowd may lead to nothing or it may lead to a stampede with people getting crushed, despite nobody wanting this or acting intentionally to produce it. Likewise no one decides to precipitate a financial crisis, and indeed at the level of the individual firms, decisions generally are made to take prudent action to avoid the costly effects of a crisis. But what is locally stable can become globally unstable.

The third characteristic "non-ergodicity", comes from German physicist Ludwig Boltzmann who defined as "ergodic" a concept in statistical mechanics whereby a single trajectory, continued long enough at constant energy, would be representative of an isolated system as a whole, from the Greek "ergon", energy, and "odos", path. The mechanical processes that drive of our physical world are ergodic, as are many biological processes. We can predict how a ball will move when struck without knowing how it got into its present position – past doesn't matter. But the past matters in social processes and you cannot simply extrapolate it to know the future. The dynamics of a financial crisis are not reflected in the pre-crisis period for instance because financial markets are constantly innovating, so the future may look nothing like the past.

Radical uncertainty completes our quartet. It describes surprises—outcomes or events that are unanticipated, that cannot be put into a probability distribution because they are outside our list of things that might occur. Electric power or the internet are examples from the past, and of course we don't know what the future will be. As Keynes put it, "There is no scientific basis to form any calculable probability whatever. We simply do not know." Economists also talk about "Knightian uncertainty", after Frank Knight, who distinguished between risk, for example gambling in a casino where we don't know the outcome but can calculate the odds; and "true uncertainty" where we can't know everything that would be needed to calculate the odds. This in fact is the human condition. We don't know where we are going, and we don't know who we will be when we get there. The reality of humanity means that a mechanistic approach to economics will fail.

So is there any hope of understanding what's happening in our irreducible, emergent, non-ergodic, radically uncertain economy? Yes, if we use methods that are more robust, that are not embedded in the standard rational expectations, optimisation mode of economics. To deal with crises, we need methods that deal with computational irreducibility; recognise emergence; allow for the fact that not even the present is reflected in the past, never mind the future; and that can deal with radical uncertainty. Agent-based modelling could be a step in the right direction.

Agent-based models (ABM) use a dynamic system of interacting, autonomous agents to allow macroscopic behaviour to emerge from microscopic rules. The models specify rules that dictate how agents act based on various inputs. Each agent individually assesses its situation and makes decisions on the basis of its rules. Starlings swirling in the sky is a good illustration. The birds appear to operate as a system, yet the flight is based on the decisions of the individual birds. Building a macro, top-down model will miss the reality of the situation, because at the macro level the movements of the flock are complex, non-linear, yet are not based on any system-wide programme. But you can model the murmuration based on simple rules as to how a bird reacts to the distance, speed and direction of the other birds, and heads for the perceived centre of the flock in its immediate neighbourhood.

Likewise, the agent-based approach recognises that individuals interact and thereby change the environment, leading to the next interaction. It operates without the fiction of a representative consumer or investor who is as unerringly right as a mathematical model can dream. It allows for construction of a narrative—unique to the particular circumstances in the real world—in which the system may jump the tracks and career down the mountainside. This narrative gives us a shot at pulling the system back safely.

In short, agent-based economics arrives ready to face the real world, the world that is amplified and distorted during times of crisis. This is a new paradigm rooted in pragmatism and in the complexities of being human.

For the financial system, we model liquidity, leverage and concentration. We plug in values we believe to accurately represent the current state of economic market. We run simulations to see how often things go off the rails. If things don't go off the rails often we make it green, if not we make it red. If you increase both liquidity and leverage, things tend to get worse. When we model risk in time according to static models, scenarios of crisis and boom are equally likely. When we apply ABM, crisis and boom are not symmetrical. Crisis is not a single bad draw from a homogeneous distribution of risks. It causes a cascade.

In the analytic deductive approach, you plan everything from start to finish and then fill it all in. This is not the way to approach a crisis where the unexpected will always happen. A better way is the "headlights on the road" approach. You go ahead and see where the next curve is. Once you get there, you see where the following curve is, and so on. You solve it as far as you can see, and you are always adapting. In a crisis, you should be able to make changes, test critical assumptions and variables.

Sources

NAEC seminar "The end of theory", OECD, 29 June 2017, http://www.oecd.org/naec/events/the-end-of-theory-financial-crises-failure-of-economics-and-sweep-of-human-interaction.htm

"Agent-based models to help economics do a better job", Richard Bookstaber, OECD Insights, http://oecdinsights.org/2017/01/23/agent-based-models-to-help-economics-do-a-better-job/

6. How can physics help economics?

Jean-Philippe Bouchaud

The crisis put classical economics under pressure. In theory, deregulated markets should be efficient, with rational agents quickly correcting any mispricing or forecasting error. Prices should reflect the underlying reality and ensure optimal allocation of resources. These "equilibrated" markets should be stable: crises can only be triggered by acute exogenous disturbances not the market itself. This is in stark contrast with most financial crashes.

The crisis might offer an occasion for a paradigm change, to which physics could contribute, through so-called econophysics. Econophysics has tended to concentrate on financial markets, and these represent an ideal laboratory for testing economics concepts using the terabytes of data generated every day by financial markets to compare theories with observations.

In financial markets, physicists are intrigued by a number of phenomena described by power-laws. For example, the distribution of price changes, of company sizes, of individual wealth all have a power-law tail, to a large extent universal. The activity and volatility of markets have a power-law correlation in time, reflecting their intermittent nature, obvious to the naked eye. Many complex physical systems display very similar intermittent dynamics, for example velocity fluctuations in turbulent flows. While the exogenous driving force is regular and steady, the resulting endogenous dynamics is complex and jittery. In these cases, the non-trivial (physicists say "critical") nature of the dynamics comes from collective effects: individual components have a relatively simple behaviour, but interactions lead to new, emergent phenomena. The whole is fundamentally different from any of its sub-parts. The dynamics of financial markets, and more generally of economic systems, may reflect the same underlying mechanisms.

Several economically-inspired models exhibit these critical features. One (a transposition of the Random Field Ising Model, RFIM) describes situations where there is a conflict between personal opinions, public information, and social pressure. Traders are influenced by some slowly varying global factors, for example interest rates or dividend forecasts. Assume no shocks in the dynamics of these exogenous factors, but that each trader is influenced by the opinion of the majority. If all agents made up their mind in isolation (zero herding tendency) then the aggregate opinion would faithfully track the external influences and, by assumption, evolve smoothly.

But if the herding tendency exceeds some finite threshold, the evolution of the aggregate opinion jumps discontinuously from optimistic to pessimistic, while global factors only deteriorate slowly and smoothly. Furthermore, some hysteresis appears. Like supersaturated vapour refusing to turn into liquid, optimism is self-consistently maintained. To trigger the crash, global factors have to degrade far beyond the point where pessimism should prevail. Likewise, these factors must improve much beyond the crash tipping point for global optimism to be reinstalled.

The representative agent theory amounts to replacing an ensemble of heterogeneous and interacting agents by a unique representative one, but in the RFIM, this is impossible: the behaviour of the crowd is fundamentally different from that of any single individual.

Minority Games define another, much richer, family of models in which agents learn to compete for scarce resources. A crucial aspect here is that the decisions of these agents impact the market: the price does not evolve exogenously but moves as a result of these decisions. A remarkable result here is the existence of a phase transition as the number of speculators increases, between a predictable market where agents can make some profit from their strategies, and an over-crowded market, where these profits vanish or become too risky.

There are other examples in physics and computer science where competition and heterogeneities lead to interesting phenomena, for example cases where even if an equilibrium state exists in theory, it may be totally irrelevant in practice, because the equilibration time is far too long.

As models become more realistic, analytics often has to give way to numerical simulations. This is well-accepted in physics, but many economists are still reluctant to recognise that numerical investigation of a model, although very far from theorem proving, is a valid way to do science. It is surprising how easily numerical experiments allow one to qualify an agent-based model (ABM) as potentially realistic or completely off the mark. What makes this expeditious diagnosis possible is the fact that for large systems details do not matter much – only a few microscopic features end up surviving at the macro scale.

The attraction of ABM is that they can put together simple elements that produce rich behaviours. The instability mechanisms in the complex systems they are used to study show common features. Phase diagrams are a core element of this approach, allowing the study of places where behaviour can change suddenly and radically. In ABM, macro observables such as output are not smooth functions of the parameters. The interest rate for example can induce a transition between a good and a bad phase.

The notion of emergence is important in ABM. Equilibrium output level is usually exogenous in traditional, models, but in an ABM it is the result of the ability of agents (or firms) to co-operate, so it is an emergent property that can appear or disappear suddenly. This is one way to think about crises.

ABM also allow for the notion of hysteresis. Different states of the economy can coexist in the same region of parameter space. The economy can be stuck in a good or a bad state, while the system could have chosen another outcome if the history had been different or some anecdotal event occurred.

ABM can allow policy experiments, even if they still require a lot of work as policy tools. They show that policies that would be stabilising if you assume infinitely rational, forward-looking agents can actually be destabilising when you remove that assumption. This makes it intrinsically difficult to design hybrid models incorporating some elements of ABM. If you abandon infinitely forward-looking agents, things happen that would not happen with them. In addition, there is the "curse of complexity". Optimised complex systems are often on the verge of instability – optimality and instability go hand in hand.

Other empirical results, useful analytical methods and numerical tricks have been established by econophysics, which I have no space to review here, but the most valuable contribution may be methodological nature. Physics constructs models of reality based on a subtle mixture of intuition, analogies and mathematical spin, where the ill-defined concept of plausibility can be more relevant than the accuracy of the prediction. Kepler's ellipses and Newton's gravitation were more plausible than Ptolemy's epicycles, even when the latter theory, after centuries of fixes and stitches, was initially more accurate to describe observations. Physicists definitely want to know what an equation means in intuitive terms, and believe that assumptions ought to be both plausible and compatible with observations. This is probably the most urgently needed paradigm shift in economics.

Sources

NAEC seminar with Olivier Blanchard "Rethinking macroeconomic policy", OECD, 5 July 2018 http://www.oecd.org/naec/events/rethinking-macroeconomic-policy.htm

The (unfortunate) complexity of the economy, Jean-Philippe Bouchaud, Physics World, April 2009, p.28-32 https://arxiv.org/abs/0904.0805v1

7. What causes financial crises?

Steve Keen

One popular explanation of financial crises is excessive government debt and spending. Historical data going back two centuries reveal serious flaws in this argument, though. Government debt was falling before two major crises and started to rise after them, and even fell to zero before the 1837 crisis, and did not rise after it. Financial crises are caused by a boom-bust process driven by private credit: excessive private debt and credit before crisis, negative credit during it (the annual change in private debt being negative rather than positive). Private debt was rising before three great crises and started to fall after the crises began. There was negative credit in the 1837 crisis, as well as in 1929 and 2007.

Fluctuations in credit are of minor significance when private debt levels are low, but are catastrophic when they are high. The mechanism starts from the fact that expenditure is income. What you spend becomes income for someone else. There are two sources of expenditure: turnover of existing money; and new money created by exports exceeding imports, governments spending more than they tax, and banks lending more than they get back in repayments. Booms are caused by bank lending, as extra credit-money is spent into the economy. Bust follows when growth in private debt stops. Credit is not the largest component of expenditure but it is by far the most volatile. A fall in credit can cause crisis even if other factors are still growing, with the effect depending on both level and rate of change of private debt. We can see this by looking at a low-debt and a high-debt example.

In the low debt ratio example, imagine an economy with turnover of existing money of USD 1000 billion/year initially, growing at 10%/year. Private debt is initially 50% of turnover of existing money, USD 500 billion, growing at 20%/year. Credit is USD 100 billion/year. Total demand is USD 1100 billion/year. The next year, turnover of existing money is USD 1100 billion; growth of debt is 10%/year; credit = USD 60 billion/year (10% of USD 600 billion); total demand is USD 1160 billion/year: USD 60 billion higher than previous year.

For the high debt ratio example, we start with the same figures, except that private debt initially is not 50% but 200% of turnover of existing money, so USD 2000 billion, growing at 20%/year, meaning credit is USD 400 billion rather than USD 100 billion/year. Total demand is now USD 1400bn/year and turnover of existing money the next year is USD 1100 billion/year. Growth of debt slows to 10%/year. Credit is USD 240 billion/year (10% of USD 2400 billion). Total demand is higher than the low debt example, USD 1340 billion versus USD 1160/year, but this is USD 60 billion lower than the previous year in the high debt scenario.

Both the level of private debt/GDP ratio and rate of growth matter. The danger zone is when private debt is greater than 150% of GDP, and credit accounts for a large fraction of total demand (10% of GDP). The data on this for recent crises are overwhelming. Japan (the first country to suffer a serious credit crisis, back in 1990) the United States, United Kingdom, and Spain had crises when private debt reached historically unprecedented levels -150% in the United States, as high as 220% in Spain and Japan. All of these crises were preceded by credit rising to substantial levels, 20% of GDP in most cases, and almost 40% in the case of Spain (where credit is the annual change in private debt).

All involved negative credit, with Spain being the worst, with credit at negative 19% of GDP in 2013. This was unprecedented since the end of WWII for all of them except the United Kingdom, and even there, the previous negative credit events had been short-lived, whereas credit was negative for most of 2009-2015. Not only did these crises begin when the credit started to fall, the ups and downs of credit were a major determinant of economic activity at all times in every country except the United Kingdom since the 1990s.

Similar relationships exist in asset markets, and in particular, between mortgage credit and house prices. This contradicts the canons of conventional finance theory, which argues that leverage does not determine asset prices. The main determinant of the change in house prices is the change in mortgage credit. For US data, econometric testing confirms that changes in mortgage credit cause changes in house prices, rather than vice versa. The correlations between change in total household credit and change in house prices since 1970 for the other countries are respectively 0.4 for Japan, 0.6 for the United Kingdom, and 0.47 for Spain.

Data like these demand examination, but a decade after the financial crisis, mainstream economists continue to ignore them. These economists have learnt an intricate and superficially all-encompassing theory, which they believe provides not merely an explanation of the complicated reality of the economy, but also a guide as to how it can be improved. A core component of mainstream theory is the belief that one can quite literally ignore the banking system when modelling the macroeconomy. This was easy to do before 2007 since there had not been a banking crisis of this scale since the Great Depression. Voluntary blindness about the role of banks and credit in macroeconomics will give the world no warning again when another crisis approaches, not because no warning is possible, but because this wilful ignorance turns a blind eye to the very obvious causes of financial crises.

These causes are unfolding now, not at a global level but in the many countries that avoided the crisis in 2008 by continuing to accumulate more private debt. The four largest such economies are China, Canada, South Korea and Australia. Others include Singapore, Sweden, Norway and Belgium. In all of these countries, government policies led the private sector to avoid the negative credit experiences that made the 2008 crisis so severe in the United States and United Kingdom. But they accumulated even more private debt than the United States and United Kingdom in 2008. These countries will therefore experience their own, localised versions of the 2008 crisis when their credit bubbles burst. When their crises occur, virtually all the world's major economies will be caught in private debt traps. The only exceptions will be countries like Germany that have exploited huge trade surpluses to enable their private sector debt levels to fall over the last two decades.

Sources

NAEC seminar "Can we avoid another financial crisis?", OECD, 5 October 2017
http://www.oecd.org/naec/events/can-we-avoid-another-financial-crisis.htm

"Hiding in plain view: why economists can't see the obvious coming"
https://www.finance-watch.org/hiding-in-plain-view-why-economists-cant-see-the-obvious-coming

8. Financial network analysis

Sheri M. Markose

The 2007 financial crisis exposed the shortcomings of monetary economics and the regulatory framework known as Basel II. While financial innovations were progressing at a rapid rate, there was a lack of urgency to develop modelling tools capable of mapping and studying the massive interrelationships in the financial system implied by the workings of new financial products. Regulators, and other actors, had to rely on approaches dating from the period of double-digit stagflation in the 1970s and early 1980s when inflationary overheating was the sign of growing monetary and economic instability. The epochal reduction in inflation starting from about 1994 gave a semblance of calm and led to complacency.

A lack of a holistic perspective on the linkages between constituent elements can be blamed for why Basel II regulatory authorities encouraged bank behaviour that may appear sound at an individual level but contributes to system-wide failure. Systemic risk in financial systems, like environmental externalities which lead to overuse and degradation of resources, arises from design problems that are required to attenuate individual behaviour based on local incentives to prevent system collapse.

ICT based multi-agent financial network models can be useful in monitoring and analysing existing systems and can be used as computational test beds for the design of robust policy reforms. They can compensate for the weaknesses of mainstream macroeconomic or monetary models for policy that show an absence of the endemic arms race of strategic gaming by those regulated, and the weaknesses of econometric models that cannot handle structural interconnections and interactions between economic units.

Network models are increasingly being used to obtain a better understanding of stability of systems in biology, eco-systems, road transport, infrastructure and cities, engineering, power networks, information systems, etc. Network analysis and fine-grained firm level data based multi-agent simulators can also help address stability concerns for any financial market. Typically, in a financial network, the nodes are financial institutions and there are links called in-degrees which represent obligations from others, while out-degrees represent a financial entity's obligations to others.

Network models depict causal chains between nodes rather than relying solely on statistical correlations which still remain the basis of most contagion models. The study of causal chains of network interconnections with nodes taken to be 'agents' with capacity for rule-based behaviour or fully autonomous behaviour that represents financial intermediaries (FIs) and regulatory authorities, constitutes the framework of financial network modelling.

The contractual obligations between FIs, and FIs and end users that determine bilateral flows of payoffs, constitute pre-existing network structures. A crisis with default of counterparties can trigger further contingent claims and large losses at default due to collapse in asset markets. Interactions of agents produce system-wide feedback loops. In the traditional equation-oriented analyses, structural changes from strategic behaviour and tracing of causal links and influences of feedback loops on individual decisions are almost impossible to do. In agent-based models, these need not be restricted to pre-specified equations that have to be estimated using past data in econometric or time series approaches. Agent-based ICT technology embedded in fine-grained digital maps of the structural interconnections of financial markets should therefore be developed as the starting point of stress tests and scenario analysis, especially in the context of the policy design.

Financial networks are not random and are most likely to have network properties like other socio-economic, communication and information networks. These manifest a statistical signature of complex systems, namely, a top tier multi-hub of few agents who are highly connected among themselves and to other nodes that show few if any connections to others in the periphery. The consequence of the clustered structure of a network is short path lengths between a node and any other node in the system. This is efficient in terms of liquidity and informational flows in good times, but worsens fragility in bad times when so-called hub banks ('super-spreaders') fail or suffer illiquidity. Failure of a big unit increases the probability of failure of other big units, an aspect of the too-interconnected-to-fail phenomenon. Structurally, however, the interconnected hubs can contain the liquidity shocks and prevent them from going to the extremities, but only if there are adequate buffers.

The presence of highly-connected and contagion-causing players typical of a complex system network perspective is to be contrasted with what economists regard to be an equilibrium network. In the latter, the probability that a contagion occurs conditional on one bank failing is significantly reduced, but the drivers of network formation in the real world are different from those assumed in economic equilibrium models. In terms of propagation of failure, however, it is not true that financial systems where no node is too interconnected are necessarily easier to manage in terms of structural coherence and stability. Stability analysis shows that the less-interconnected system is in some respects more dangerous. This suggests the need for caution in espousing an ideal network topology for financial networks.

It is important to consider network formation to be a complex adaptive process in that nodes interact strategically and respond to institutional incentives. A key aspect of complex adaptive systems is the capacity of interacting agents to show über intelligence with strong proclivities for contrarian (rule breaking) behaviour and the production of structure changing novelty and 'surprises'. This takes the co-evolutionary form of a regulator-regulatee arms race with monitoring and production of countervailing new measures by the authorities in response to regulatee deviations from rules due to perverse incentives or loopholes. Failure to monitor and co-evolve the regulatory framework by authorities could result in system collapse.

Instability of large networks can result from a combination of individually rational behaviour and policy incentives which reinforce local efficiency but cause an increase in concentration and interconnectedness in the form of closer coupling with reduced buffers of nodes to a point of supercriticality or instability. The pressure to conserve scarce resources can lead to buffers being treated as costly and superfluous, leading to tighter coupling within the system. Economic forces can drive both designed and self-organising systems towards being balanced on the point of supercriticality where extreme system failure can follow. In the financial system, the different ways by which FIs in the system implement avoidance or reduction of key buffers (capital, collateral and margin requirements, for example) plus the numbers of those doing this have implications for the size of the hub nodes, the inter-connectivity between them and smaller nodes, and also contingent feedback loops of the system. All these factors can move the system to a supercritical state.

Socio-economic system failures, including financial crises, arise from a disparity between the pursuit of local interest and those needed for overall stability of the system. Poor rules made with no cognizance of their systemic risk consequences can wreck financial superstructures faster than any terrorist malfeasance.

Sources

NAEC seminar "Systemic Risk Analysis in Finance: New Approaches and Tools", OECD, 9 September 2013

"Multi-Agent Financial Network Analyses For Systemic Risk Management Post-2007 Financial Crisis: A New Complexity Perspective for G10 and BRICs", Sheri Markose, et al., Research Gate, 2010 https://www.researchgate.net/publication/267766719

9. Economics after the crisis: Three learnings and three trilemmas

Maurice Obstfeld

The crisis taught us three lessons, but these were there to be learned even before 2008: finance is central to macroeconomic outcomes; multiple equilibria can be all-important under stressful conditions; and the political economy of policy matters. The processes that would precipitate the fall of Lehman Brothers and provoke the crisis were already at work decades before in Asia and Latin America. There were even warnings about the rise of anti-globalist sentiment if those who lost out only had nationalism to turn to.

The crisis also highlighted three trilemmas, one monetary, one financial and one political. The classic monetary "trilemma" (a word coined by Friedman) postulates that countries face a trade-off among the objectives of exchange rate stability, free capital mobility, and independent monetary policy. If a country chooses exchange rate stability and free capital mobility, it must give up monetary policy autonomy; conversely, an independent monetary policy in the presence of free capital flows is possible through exchange rate flexibility. The rise in cross-border capital flows over the past few decades, and the frequent boom-bust cycles in capital flows, have however put the trilemma to the test and doubts have been raised about the ability of countries with flexible exchange rates to insulate their financial conditions from changes in key-currency financial centres.

In an alternative view, cross-border financial spillovers are similar for fixed and flexible exchange rate countries, implying the irrelevance of the exchange rate regime, and a two-way trade-off between capital mobility and monetary autonomy (Rey's policy "dilemma" rather than a trilemma). According to this argument, regardless of the currency regime, monetary autonomy cannot insulate countries, so they need to use macroprudential policies, or failing that, capital controls.

There is however strong evidence from the response of a range of domestic financial variables to global financial conditions across exchange rate regimes in 43 emerging market economies that floating rates do provide a degree of insulation even from foreign financial shocks. In particular, exchange rate flexibility successfully dampens the magnitude of the cross-border transmission to domestic credit growth, real estate prices, and financial sector leverage. Global investor risk aversion shocks are transmitted more strongly through cross-border flows when the recipient countries have relatively inflexible exchange rate regimes and most emerging economies that have chosen a resolution of the monetary trilemma based on exchange rate flexibility have gained.

However, the bigger problem is the enhanced difficulty of effective financial policy in an open economy: the Schoenmaker or financial trilemma: financial stability, financial integration and national financial policies are incompatible at the same time. For example, strict rules on subprime lending have little impact if foreign banks still lend to these individuals. One response has been greater use of macroprudential policy, but this is not the whole answer and there are moves to improve international regulation as well as more questioning of the benefits from international capital movements and more openness to thinking about measures that target capital flows.

These flows are an integral component of multiple equilibria. While the classic literature focused on bank runs or currency crises, the 1980s Asian crisis highlighted "twin" crises, banking plus currency. But multiple equilibria are not just an emerging market pathology. The 2008 crisis showed the importance not only of bank runs, but of the flight of short-term wholesale funding from non-banks. The euro area crisis showed how sovereign debt could also be subject to multiple equilibria and the importance of feedback loops, non-linearity and other complex phenomena. Financial stability requires a fiscally strong sovereign, and sovereign weakness can undermine faith in financial safety net. Banking or financial system weakness may lead to government support, but if markets feel that government finances are too weak to carry the extra burden, interest rates will go up, making the burden even heavier and leading to sovereign debt worries. The sudden shifts this provokes between equilibria is a highly non-linear effect that cannot be accommodated in linear macroeconomic models.

This "doom loop" between fiscal weakness and financial fragility is illustrated by three problems: fiscal weakness worsens slumps because the government interventions lack sufficient means; the slump makes the fiscal situation worse and resources used for any interventions further reduce fiscal space to react to future crises; and recessions have hysteresis effects – the impact of the crisis on productivity lasts many years after the crisis ends.

The crisis also has political impacts, influenced by the fact that median real incomes have grown slowly or stagnated and inequality of income and wealth has increased in many countries (although these trends pre-date the crisis). While there is discussion of whether job dislocation; de-industrialisation; and the splits between high and low skill workers, urban and rural areas, and mobile and immobile workers are due to primarily to globalisation, technology, or policies, it is clear that these developments have fuelled resentment against traditional elites and "experts", and the continued political power of financial interests, that finds expression in various populist and nationalistic movements.

This resentment can be translated into hostility against emerging and developing country economies, whose growth is outstripping that of the advanced economies. This is one factor making global co-operation harder and focussing attention on the Rodrik trilemma which says that at most two out of the following three are compatible: democracy; national policy autonomy; and extensive globalisation. The "sweet spot" where all three can coexist requires an inclusive policy framework such that most people gain from globalisation, even if inequality persists (as has been the case in many emerging and developing country economies). But designing and implementing such a framework is endogenous to voter choices, and there is no guarantee they would choose it.

So somewhat paradoxically, by helping emerging economies to succeed and thereby reducing the relative importance of the advanced economies, globalisation has threatened its own sustainability, and the future of multilateral co-operation. The challenge for economists is to find the best policies in the face of past and future structural transformation and to convince the public and politicians to adopt them. Scientific rigor remains necessary, but it is no longer sufficient. In 1924, another turbulent period, Keynes put it this way: the economist must be "as aloof and incorruptible as an artist, yet sometimes as near to earth as a politician".

Sources

"10 Years after the failure of Lehman Brothers: What have we learned?" NAEC Conference, OECD, 13-14 September 2018, http://www.oecd.org/naec/10-years-after-the-crisis/

"Trilemmas and Tradeoffs: Living with Financial Globalization" BIS Working papers N°480, January 2015 https://www.bis.org/publ/work480.pdf

10. Narrative economics

Robert Shiller

Narrative economics is based on the premise that narratives are not just a way describing and seeking to understand what has happened, but that stories that "go viral" evolve to actually affect outcomes, including crises, depressions, and recessions. The narrative basis of economic phenomena might be hard to see since narratives are not easy to measure, but by incorporating an understanding of popular narratives into their explanations, economists will become more sensitive to such influences and may produce better forecasts. For the last half century, one-year forecasts have been worthless on the whole.

Two elements are particularly important to narrative economics: word-of-mouth contagion of ideas in the form of stories; and people's efforts to generate new contagious stories or make existing stories more contagious. An economic narrative reminds people of facts they may have forgotten, explains how things work in the economy, and affects how people think about the justification or purpose of economic actions. Seven propositions are key to economic narratives.

1. The timetable and magnitude of economic narrative epidemics can vary widely.
2. Narratives may be rarely heard and still economically important. People may not talk much about important the important economic decisions that are given a lot of attention in the media, but they will discuss the effects and fears they associate with the economy. During the Great Depression, for example, stories of hard-working people having to eat from garbage cans were contagious.
3. Narrative constellations have more impact than any one narrative, for instance stories around cryptocurrency featuring people who made fortunes from Bitcoin or would have made fortunes if they'd held on to them.
4. The economic impact of narratives may change through time, and we must resist the temptation to assume that all the narratives featuring the same words mean the same years apart.
5. Truth is not enough to stop false narratives.
6. Reinforcement matters, and the contagion of economic narratives builds on opportunities for repetition.
7. Economic narratives thrive on human interest, identity and patriotism.

The first narrative of the Great Depression was that of the stock market drop on October 28, 1929. This narrative was especially powerful, in its suddenness and severity, focusing public attention on a crash as never before in America. But, beyond the record size, it is hard to say what made this crash narrative such a success that it persists today. Part of the strength seems to come from a certain moralising. Sermons preached on the Sunday after the crash attributed it to moral and spiritual excesses, helping frame a narrative of a sort of day-of-judgment on the "Roaring Twenties."

Another narrative at the beginning of the Great Depression was that of a repeat of the 1920-21 crash. For the general public, this would be falling prices, so it made sense to delay purchases. Economists expected the contraction to be as short lived as in 1920-21, which helps explain why President Hoover and others confidently explained that it would be over soon. But the public didn't necessarily believe the President. Economists should look more at testimonies of women to understand the consumption function, and how they decided on shopping strategies, particularly since shopping was mainly a woman's role.

Even as it happened, the contraction was thought of popularly as the product of some kind of feedback, famously tackled by President Roosevelt stating "the only thing to fear is fear itself". Roosevelt took the unusual step of addressing the nation on the radio at a time of a massive national bank run that had necessitated shutting all the banks. In this "fireside chat" he explained the banking crisis and asked people not to continue their demands on banks. His personal request ended the run and money flowed into, not out of, the banks when they reopened. The narrative of this first fireside chat is still with us today, but the narrative has not been powerful enough, or not used well enough, to prevent recessions.

The macro storyline in the Great Depression gradually morphed into a national revulsion against the excesses of the Roaring Twenties. Contagion rates for stories of business failures, rather than inspirational stories, were naturally high at a time of high unemployment. Other narratives focused on the rising leftist or communist movement. The increasing radicalisation of President Roosevelt plays a part in these stories: in 1936, speaking of the magnates of organised money, he said "I welcome their hatred".

Financial crises like 2008 are also driven by stories. Stories about bank runs in the 19th century were virtually synonymous with financial crises. After the Great Depression bank runs were thought to be cured, but the run on Northern Rock in 2007, the first UK bank run since 1866, brought back the old narratives of panicked depositors forming angry crowds outside closed banks. The story led to a nervousness internationally, and in 2008 to the Washington Mutual bank run in the United States, and the Reserve Prime Fund run a few days after that. These events then led to the very unconventional US government guarantee of all US money market funds for a year. Governments were aware that they could not let the old story of a bank run go live over concern for its effects on public anxiety.

Naming the financial crisis after the Great Depression was not the choice of any one individual. There had been earlier unsuccessful attempts to attach the name "Great Recession" to preceding recessions, so what is it about the 2007-9 event that made the name "Great Recession" suddenly contagious? Judging from the peak US unemployment rate, it was less severe than the 1981-82 recession. Perhaps it was because the 2007-9 event fitted the most generic and ill-informed memories of the Great Depression. People remember massive bank failures as part of the Great Depression story, and that was a better fit with the events of 2007. In the 1981-82 recession the stock market had not been booming, and the stock market did not fall below its 1980 value by 1982. In contrast, 2007-9 saw a near halving of the market from very high levels. People in 1981-82 were preoccupied with out-of-control consumer-price inflation, and saw the events in terms of a suddenly strong central bank effort to contain the inflation.

The Great Depression is exaggerated in people's minds because of its legendary status. In 2007-09 presidents and prime ministers invoked parallels to the Great Depression to justify their requests to apply stimulus. Did this contribute to a self-fulfilling prophecy, a mirror event to the Great Depression, albeit not as severe (Great Recession, not Great Depression)? However, no politician can actually control the progression of the narratives they create. The manner in which these narratives unfold will play an important role in any economic forecast. To best predict economic activity, we need, among other things, to watch the narratives and ask: how will the emerging twists in the narratives affect propensity to spend, to start unconventional new businesses, to hire new employees? In short, how will the animal spirits be affected?

Sources

NAEC seminar "Narrative economics", OECD, 10 September 2019,
http://www.oecd.org/naec/events/narrative-economics.htm

"Narrative Economics," Robert J. Shiller, American Economic Review, vol 107(4), 2017, pages 967-1004

Narrative Economics: How Stories Go Viral and Drive Major Economic Events, Robert J. Shiller,
Princeton University Press, 2019

11. Simple lessons for macro policymakers from embracing complexity

William White

"It is worse than a crime. It is a mistake."
Joseph Fouche

"We have gotten into a terrible muddle. We have blundered in the operations of a delicate machine, the workings of which we do not understand."
John Maynard Keynes

The grave problems now facing the global economy have been building up over many decades. In large part they are the by-product of well intentioned but mistaken macroeconomic policies, themselves based on mistaken assumptions about the nature of the global economy. A philosopher would say policymakers have made a fundamental ontological error. Changing those underlying beliefs, and thus avoiding the disastrous effects of "still more of the same" macroeconomic policies, is the biggest challenge now faced by policymakers.

The analytical framework used by policymakers assumes that the economy can be adequately represented by linear models that are essentially simple and static. Moreover, the economy is assumed to tend rather mechanistically towards an "equilibrium" which has properties the policymakers want - like full employment. The economy is therefore understandable and easily controllable. Really bad outcomes are ruled out by assumption.

Unfortunately, this framework is fundamentally mistaken, as events over the last decade have shown. The economy is actually a complex, adaptive system (CAS) which is constantly evolving, never in equilibrium and has highly non-linear properties. Fortunately, CAS are ubiquitous in both nature and society, and how best to manage them has been well been studied by many disciplines. Still more fortunately, such systems share many basic characteristics. This communality implies that insights from other disciplines might be speedily applied to macroeconomic policies as well. Ironically, the conceptual embrace of complexity leads to at least ten lessons for policymakers that are actually quite simple.

Lesson 1: **Policymakers' multiple objectives make trade-offs inevitable.** CAS break down on a regular basis, determined by Power Laws, so policy must always trade off efficiency against sustainability and system resilience. Macroeconomic polices must also take note of their implications for the distribution of income and wealth. Such considerations affect the transmission mechanism of macro policies and have important spillover effects into even more complex social and political systems.

Lesson 2: **Policymakers can affect structure, and structure matters.** While a CAS will have its own evolutionary dynamic, policy induced structural changes can make it easier to achieve desired objectives. It is well known that structural reforms can increase static efficiency. It seems less well known that buffers, redundancy and modularity can increase resilience. Unnecessary complexity should be stripped away.

Lesson 3: **Policymakers should minimax not maximise.** Our understanding of CAS will always be incomplete. Thus, optimisation is beyond our powers. Rather, since systemic breakdowns can have extremely bad outcomes, policy should focus more heavily on trying to avoid such outcomes. The use of highly experimental policies (and new products) should be constrained by the "do no harm" principle which guides both medical doctors and drug administrations.

Lesson 4: **Policymakers should act more symmetrically.** CAS are all path dependent and therefore "where you are" conditions "where you can go". Stocks of debt built up over time make the economy increasingly fragile in all states of nature, both inflationary and deflationary. To avoid such buildups both monetary and fiscal policies should lean against upturns as strongly as they lean against downturns. Private sector debt exposures should be further limited by revoking interest deductibility for tax purposes as well as share buybacks.

Lesson 5: **Policymakers should expect the unexpected**. Because CAS are "adaptive", policymakers are always in danger of fighting the last war. Worse, their own policies often encourage changes (regulatory evasion and moral hazard) that lead to this outcome. "Whack a mole" is not a strategy.

Lesson 6: **Policymakers should focus on systemic risks more than "triggers".** In a highly stressed CAS, almost anything could be the trigger for a crisis. It is far more important to develop indicators of growing risks to systemic stability. That said, new financial products often "trigger" broader problems.

Lesson 7: **Policymakers should be guided by multiple indicators.** In a CAS, many things can go wrong. The belief that Consumer Price Index (CPI) "price stability" is sufficient to ensure macroeconomic stability is a false belief. Similarly, "financial stability" (the stability of the financial sector) is also insufficient since problems (like rising corporate debt or household debt) can arise outside of the financial system.

Lesson 8: **Policymakers cannot forecast.** In CAS, the future is essentially unknowable. While such systems can remain stable for long periods, a prediction that they will continue to do so is simply unwarranted extrapolation. Instead of decimal point forecasts, it would be better to provide alternative scenarios based on an assessment of emerging threats to systemic stability. This would also serve to remind people that radical uncertainty is a central characteristic of CAS. This implies the need for much larger buffers than are implied by traditional risk assessment procedures.

Lesson 9: **Policymakers should be prepared for breakdowns.** Since crises are inevitable in CAS, policymakers should prepare beforehand. "War games" should be played regularly, recognising that crises can start and unfold in myriad ways. Memoranda of Understanding between different policymakers should be negotiated and agreed. Legislation to ensure orderly insolvencies (for corporates, households and financial institutions) needs to be enacted. Since crises can vary in myriad ways, it is important that the authorities have the flexibility required to respond adequately.

Lesson 10: **No policymaker is an island**. By definition, CAS are defined by their interdependencies. All national policymakers must therefore formulate their policies with a view to the effects on other national policymakers and their responses. Such considerations evidently limit the "independence" of central banks and of national regulatory agencies. Moreover, since the interdependencies are increasingly international, this raises questions about the viability of policies directed purely to national objectives. Embracing complexity requires a review of the existing International Monetary (Non) System.

Economists are fond of saying "It takes a model to replace a model". We now have such a model. The economy is a complex, adaptive system and should be treated as such. The ten practical lessons for policymakers, described above, are simple but revolutionary. That is precisely why they should be adopted. We need a paradigm shift to get off our current disastrous path. If we continue to pursue relentlessly the impeccable logic of an argument which is based on false assumptions, it will be worse than a crime. It will be a mistake.

12. Modern central banking: conventional and unconventional measures from 2008 to Covid-19

Matheus Grasselli

Looking back 10 years after the last crisis, several participants in the NAEC conference that took place in September 2018, myself included, expressed concern that, when the next crisis inevitably hit, central banks would find themselves much more constrained in their response, for both regulatory and political reasons. Covid-19 showed that these concerns were spectacularly misplaced: central banks around the world did more in a few weeks to contain the fallout from the pandemic than they had done in several months following the 2008 crisis and its aftermath.

Key measures of financial distress, began to increase in late February 2020 and headed to crisis territory in early March, when it became clear that the pandemic would cause widespread disruptions in the world economy. Stock markets experienced gyrations of such rapidity that even automatic circuit breakers were not fast enough to halt losses. The financial press ran out of nicknames for crash days: Black Monday I (March 9) was followed by Black Thursday (March 12) and then Black Monday II (March 16) – each breaking records set in previous crises.

As governments were enacting measures to contain a rapidly spreading virus, central banks sprang into action to prevent the spread of an even faster contagion in financial markets. In what follows, I focus on the measures taken by the Federal Reserve, but similar stories can be told about the Bank of England, the ECB, and other major central banks.

The first line of defence of central banks in a crisis is to accelerate conventional monetary policy. And accelerate the Fed did: in two consecutive rate cuts in as many weeks, it brought the policy rate down by 150 basis points to its lowest possible corridor above zero. By comparison, it took the Fed 9 months and 4 rate cuts between March and December 2008 to lower the policy rate from 2.25% to effectively zero.

The next line of defence consists of a central bank assuming the role of lender-of-last-resort (LOLR) for solvent banks and financial institutions facing immediate funding liquidity shortages. The traditional "discount window" falls into this category and has been renamed by the Fed as Primary Credit, Secondary Credit, and Seasonal Credit, depending on the institutions that have access to it and the rates charged. The use of these facilities spiked immediately after the Lehman weekend, rising at a pace of approximately USD 100 billion per week and peaking at about USD 450 billion on October 15, 2008. This was the same pace of expansion observed in mid-March 2020; however, the discount window was further extended by the creation of the Term Asset-Backed Securities Loan Facility offering non-recourse loans to issuers of asset-backed securities (with a non-resource loan, the lender cannot claim the assets of the borrower other than those used as collateral). In so doing, the Fed extended its role as LOLR to traditional depository institutions to include a much larger array of eligible borrowers than in 2008.

An essential feature of global markets highlighted by the 2008 crisis was that, because foreign banks have disproportionate quantities of dollar-denominated liabilities, global funding liquidity shortages are essentially shortages of US dollars. To address this, the Fed made extensive use of swap lines with a select group of central banks in 2008, peaking at slightly less than USD 600 billion. These swap lines have remained in place since then, reaching a level of about USD 100 billion during the Euro crisis in early 2012, though they were rarely used in following years. One of the key question marks about international financial co-operation in the Trump era has been the extent to which swap lines would be used again in the next crisis. The response to Covid-19 put this question to rest: swap lines were extended to a total of 14 central banks, including those of Brazil, Mexico, and South Korea, and quickly reached their legal maximum of USD 450 billion, where they currently sit.

A novel aspect of central bank response in 2008 was the role of dealer-of-last-resort (DOLR). This was a consequence of the integration of modern banking and finance into what Perry Mehrling describes as "money market funding of capital market lending". In other words, instead of intermediating between traditional loans and deposits, banks and other financial institutions are now part of a complex network of interconnected balance sheets of market-makers straddling securities deals all the way from primary savers to ultimate borrowers. Such dealers hold inventory risk and make profits on the basis of bid-ask spreads in return. The problem arises when, in a crisis, no spread is large enough for private dealers to "make" markets, which simply cease to function. By absorbing a vast array of securities in its own balance sheet, a central bank can restore the ability of these markets to operate. This type of intervention to provide market liquidity, as opposed to more traditional funding liquidity, was behind the most audacious moves made by the Fed in 2008, quite distinct from the more common rationales for quantitative easing related to interest rates. The full extent of these interventions is difficult to measure, as many were done through special purpose vehicles (SPV) whose assets do not appear on the Fed's balance sheet, but data for one of them, the Commercial Paper Funding Facility, shows interventions of the order of USD 250 billion at its maximum. This DOLR role for the Fed has made a comeback during Covid-19, with the re-opening of several 2008-era facilities and the creation of brand-new ones. For example, as part of what is being called Jeremy Powell's "whatever it takes moment", on March 23, the Fed announced a new facility, established as an SPV with equity provided by the Treasury as part of the CARES Act, with the purpose of directly purchasing corporate bonds – a move previously considered unthinkable for a central bank.

The combined results of all these measures is that, between March 6 and May 27, 2020, the Fed's balance sheet expanded by a factor of two thirds to a total size of over USD 7 trillion – an approximate pace of USD 220 billion per week, more than double the *monthly* average expansion observed in the aftermath of the 2008 crisis. In both scale and scope, then, the response to Covid-19 appears to have inaugurated a new era in modern central banking.

13. The mystery of banking: where did the money come from?

Avner Offer

Between the early 1980s and 2008 domestic credit in the United Kingdom rose about fivefold as a percentage of GDP and about half of that in the United States. The mechanics of banking indicate how this expansion might have been achieved, and who stood to gain or lose.

Contrary to intuition, the constraint on lending is not prior funding, but the need for credit-worthy borrowers. To see how, begin with a pure credit economy with a single bank. The bank lends by crediting a borrower's account, 'by the stroke of a pen', no more. When the borrower spends, the money never leaves the bank, it just moves to another account. Money is created when the bank lends, and is destroyed when repaid. The bank stands ready to lend to any reliable borrower. It has to be prudent since bad debts diminish capital and can threaten solvency. Profit arises from the real-world productivity of investment (the increment of money comes out of loans to other borrowers). If we started a banking system from scratch, this might be the model to use; if the single bank was also a central bank it could pursue macroeconomic objectives.

A bank can run out of money when there is more than one of them. The money lent out by one bank is likely to be deposited in another. For the first bank this is offset by inflows originating in loans made by its peers. Banks can create new money by lending and if they all do so at the same pace, most of it comes back with little need for extra funding. But they don't. They compete for market share. Money goes out and comes in unevenly (with leakages to cash and overseas). Outgoings and incomings are settled in central bank reserves, which banks cannot create. Banks acquire these reserves by purchasing government bonds with their own deposit money. They sell or lend the bonds to the central bank in exchange for the reserves they need.

A commercial bank must be ready to pay out at all times but a good deal of its outgoings are not under its control. Credit lines, overdrafts and deposits can be drawn down at any time so the bank needs to be sure of access to central bank reserves. The bank's own reserves there are only a thin buffer. The first line of defence are credit lines with other banks and the bank stands ready to lend any of its own surplus. If a bank cannot clear its balance, the central bank will do this automatically for a price. In the past banks used to hold a buffer of liquid assets such as commercial and treasury bills, but since the 1980s liquidity is mostly managed by borrowing short-term in the money markets. UK Banks used to keep asset maturities short but since the 1980s they are increasingly locked into more lucrative but long-maturity mortgages (American banks securitise their mortgages and sell them off). Liquidity risk and the need for funding arises from this maturity mismatch. Banks are meant to be in surplus overall but daily balance sheets can be volatile and they generate 'liquidity gaps'. The central challenge of banking is to remain liquid at the lowest cost, which is as much an art as a science.

The cash floats of households and business (held as deposits) are the largest, most reliable and cheapest source of funding. Another source of liquidity is 'shadow banking', financial institutions without central bank accounts. These insurance companies, pension funds, hedge funds, fund managers and suchlike lend more in the aggregate than the banks. The financial sector as a whole borrows more than households, non-financial corporations, and government (each separately), most of it for unproductive speculation in securities.

After the banking deregulation of the early 1980s aggregate domestic debt service has risen to an order of 10-20 percent of GDP a year, a transfer from spenders to hoarders that is more than the cost of the health service in the United Kingdom. Deregulation in the 1980s facilitated credit expansion. Before the 1980s housing was mostly funded by building societies (in the United Kingdom) and to a lesser extent by 'thrifts'

(Savings and Loans banks, in the United States). These institutions acted as intermediaries, taking cash from savers to lend out as mortgages without creating new money. House prices were kept in check by the limited supply of savings. In the 1980s commercial banks moved into housing finance but without the same prudential constraint. They could create new money. Housing is credit-worthy due to its built-in collateral, and abundant credit acts to raise its price. Shelter is an essential good, paid for out of household income, which constitutes a massive debt-service funding base. For borrowers, a rising proportion of income went into debt service, which was more than offset for them by rising house values. But debt service is self-limiting – eventually it diverts income away from consumption and employment, and instigates financial crises.

When the crises came governments and central banks took care of creditors ahead of any other group in society, with the largest outlays seen in peacetime. The banking system was forgiven its debts while governments imposed austerity on public services. Abundant credit has driven house prices beyond the reach of younger people and of those on moderate earnings. The suppression of demand by debt service, both public and private, has also held down household incomes. The consequences of these policy choices is a simmering dissatisfaction which has fed into a social and political crisis with no end in sight.

Sources

"The mystery of banking: an exploratory essay", Avner Offer, unpublished paper, July 2020. https://docs.google.com/viewer?a=v&pid=sites&srcid=ZGVmYXVsdGRvbWFpbnxhdm9mZmVyfGd4OjU 5ZDlhNzA2YjUwNWFjNTk

"The market turn: from social democracy to market liberalism", Avner Offer, Economic History Review, vol 70 (4), 2017, pages 1051-1071

2 The Role of the Financial System

This section looks at the role of central banking in the crisis and how this relates to finance. It calls for socially responsible investment management on the part of fund managers and analyses the links between inequality and rent-seeking in the financial sector. It urges greater efforts to align the financial system with sustainable development. It argues that financial bubbles can be positive as well as dangerous. The section also considers the place of currency in relation to debt and sovereignty.

14. How should we think about finance?

Atif Mian

There is a story we like to tell about the role of finance, and it goes as follows.

Ordinary people save out of their incomes but do not have the time to deploy these savings into productive investments. So they turn to financial firms such as banks that specialise in the ability to hand over the savings to productive entrepreneurs. The entrepreneur makes a healthy profit on average and shares the proceeds with savers and bankers. Thus everyone wins and lives happily ever after.

It is a feel-good story about finance and its role in the economy. But is it true?

There is no doubt that elements of the story are real. For example, at the start of 2020, U.S. banks had lent 2.35 trillion USD to firms as "commercial and industrial loans" to be utilised in the business of production. However, this traditional role of finance has been playing an increasingly shrinking role over the last few decades.

For example, total lending in the United States amounted to a whopping 47.4 trillion USD in the start of 2020. A relatively small fraction of it was used to finance productive investments of the sort we tell in our traditional story. Most of the outstanding lending, or debt, was used for non-productive purposes like financing consumption. And the share of debt used for non-productive purposes has been rising over time. Not only is the standard narrative about finance an inaccurate portrayal of reality, but it is becoming an increasingly irrelevant one.

So what *is* going on with finance? Since 1980 there has been a massive expansion in the U.S. economy's dependence on finance. Total debt was 142 percent of national output in 1980, and rose to an unprecedented 254 percent of national output by 2019. If all this additional credit were to be used for productive investment as the traditional story goes, we should have seen an explosion in investment. Instead investment share of national output *declined* from an average of 24 percent during the 1980s to 21 percent during the 2010s.

The story of the rise in finance despite stagnation in investment can only be understood in light of arguably the most important "structural break" in American society: the rising share of income going to the top 1 percent. Economists Thomas Piketty, Emmanuel Saez and Gabriel Zucman estimate that the post-tax share of income going to the top 1percent rose from 9 percent in 1980 to 15 percent in recent years. In a new working paper (Mian, Straub and Sufi (2020a), we show that the rise in inequality naturally leads to an expansion in finance because the very rich tend to save a much larger fraction of their income.

Distributional national accounts combined with consumption data show that saving by the bottom 90% of the income distribution has fallen significantly since 1980 while saving of the top 1 percent rose. We show that the financial sector intermediated this process by channelling the additional saving by the top 1 percent as household debt to the bottom 90 percent till 2008. Since 2008, the saving of the rich has increasingly been used to finance the expanding fiscal deficit.

The broader picture that emerges from this analysis is that the traditional framework of "saving equals investment" can be misleading. If investment at the macro level is not responsive to increasing availability of credit and lower interest rates, finance must find alternative mechanisms to absorb additional savings. In the past, this has happened through increased borrowing by households and governments for generally consumption purposes.

However, there is a natural limit to how far this process can go. Borrowing for consumption purposes is "non-productive" in the sense that it does not generate additional return. Hence in the absence of sufficient income growth for the borrowing population, interest rates must continue to fall in order to keep debt servicing manageable and enable borrowers to borrow more. The trouble starts when interest rate gets close to zero and it becomes harder to push on this mechanism further – at that point the economy might fall into a recession or a long period of stagnation. There are increasing signs that the global economy is suffering from such a problem.

All this raises some very important questions for researchers. How should we change our macro-finance models to better incorporate the key fact of increasing funding of non-productive demand side by the financial sector? How are structural forces such as inequality and the rise in finance related? This calls for explicit modelling of where the supply of savings comes from and the various investment and consumption margins that might facilitate absorption of these savings.

Another very important related question is figuring out why investment has not responded to both the greater availability of credit, and the large fall in long-term interest rates. Should this be seen as a "failure of finance", or is it driven by a lack of investment demand? Finally, an expanded view of finance, that opens up the possibility that a large share of finance might be used to fund non-productive spending, has important implications for tax policy, fiscal policy and monetary policy. We discuss some of these issues in Mian, Straub and Sufi (2020b), but there is a lot more that deserves attention.

Sources

Mian, Atif; Ludwig Straub and Amir Sufi, 2020a. "The Saving Glut of the Rich and the Rise in Household Debt", working paper.

Mian, Atif; Ludwig Straub and Amir Sufi, 2020b. "Indebted Demand", working paper.

15. The crisis, finance and central banking

Jean-Claude Trichet

With the benefit of hindsight, we can see that the crisis resulted from the interactions of at least five features of the world economic system. First, the extreme sophistication of financial instruments and the development of securitisation, the generalisation of derivative markets, the rapid growth of shadow banking, and the emergence of highly-leveraged institutions. We had a new financial environment that was very obscure in many respect and very difficult to decipher.

Second, we had increased interconnectedness between all financial and non-financial institutions, enabled and encouraged by the advance of information technologies, giving rise to new, untested properties of global finance. At the same time, we had what appears to be strange now, a sentiment of excessive tranquillity and confidence both in the public and private sectors due to sustained growth (even at a low level) with low inflation.

Third, we believed that were justified to speak of a Great Moderation, a permanent reduction in the volatility of business cycle fluctuations thanks to institutional and structural change.

Fourth, and linked to the Great Moderation, consensus in the international community on the efficiency of markets in almost all circumstances, justifying large deregulation. The belief that the financial system could never be far away from a single optimal equilibrium. This implied that the possibility of multiple equilibria could be neglected by market participants.

Fifth, generalised excess leverage was totally neglected by the international community before the crisis.

The first two reasons are forgivable. It was hard to capture the emerging properties of the new world until the crisis came as a kind of stress test. What is unforgivable was to be that calm when we were accumulating so much debt. And we are still vulnerable, perhaps more vulnerable at a global level today than we were in 2007 if we look at global debt to GDP ratios.

The major response to the crisis was unconventional quantitative policies, quantitative easing and the like. At the European Central Bank (ECB), and elsewhere, we had to accept that we were in an extraordinary situation. These measures were designed to combat directly, and very aggressively, a crisis creating a major disruption of all markets. That had nothing to do with the level of interest rates. It was because the markets themselves were signalling an absence of functioning. The specific actions in the United States and Europe were different because of our different financial structures. In Europe, we focused on the banks. In the United States around 75 percent of the economy was financed through markets and only twenty-five or twenty through banks, so the Fed had to provide liquidity massively to financial institutions. One consequence of the crisis could be the idea of maintaining permanently the capacity of public authorities to substitute when needed for the private sector.

A striking feature of this response to the crisis is the acceptance that you have measures that are off-balance-sheet for central banks. Telling commercial banks you can have all the liquidity you need provided you have the eligible collateral means that there is an implicit off-balance-sheet commitment of the order of four trillion euros, the amount of eligible collateral. Only a small fraction is utilised, but the commitment is there and was so extraordinary that it was neglected by observers and market participants.

The crisis saw convergence of views on the role of central banks. Before 2007, the dominant school of thought was that banking surveillance should be independent, particularly of the central bank. During and after the crisis, it was accepted that the central banks could have good reasons to be at the heart of banking surveillance or close to it. The United Kingdom changed its approach, Europe gave this responsibility to the ECB, and the US Federal Reserve System's important role was acknowledged. Convergence is not total, though, since it does not include Japan.

The second element of convergence concerns the prevention of systemic risks. Before the crisis, this was not seen as the very important concept it is now.

A third point is a change of view on monetary policy. It might seem bizarre ex-post that the dynamics of credit we are not considered important before the crisis. Nobody would claim today when deciding overall monetary policy that you can neglect the consequence on price stability of the accumulation of indebtedness.

Central banks have all converged towards much more active communication, and because of the crisis press conferences are generalised now. You have to explain tirelessly what you're doing and why you're doing it.

The last element of convergence concerns the definition of price stability. The central banks that issue four of the five currencies in the IMF's Special Drawing Right have the same definition of price stability. This has consequences in terms of stability of the international monetary system when you have different medium and long-term real growth rates.

A final issue concerns not the crisis as such, but the tools that economics gave us to understand and deal with it. In 2010, I said that as a policy-maker during the crisis, I found the available models of limited help and that in the face of the crisis, we felt abandoned by conventional tools. As the crisis unfolded after the collapse of Lehman, the figures we had were demonstrating a collapse that was out of all the ranges of traditional modelling. The models were not showing us even approximately where we were.

New non-linear considerations have to be introduced into our models. I was impressed by the fact that some things I could see with my own eyes in the financial world and in the real economy were closer to phenomena you observe in physics than what you normally observe in economics. Dynamic stochastic general equilibrium models have difficulty in capturing phase transitions for example, such as the way spreads changed suddenly after the collapse of Lehman. It was not that the market was totally disrupted, it was that the perception of risk had changed overnight. It is clear, too, that the efficient markets hypothesis cannot be accepted ex ante in all cases. We could learn a lot from econophysics in these respects.

Is the financial system still vulnerable? The pace of additional leverage at a global level has continued as before the crisis, driven by the emerging economies. In an interconnected global economy, leverage is a vulnerability indicator as to systemic instability. Today, this indicator is not reassuring.

Source

"10 Years after the failure of Lehman Brothers: What have we learned?" NAEC Conference, OECD, 13-14 September 2018, http://www.oecd.org/naec/10-years-after-the-crisis/

16. Socially responsible investment management

Thomas Coutts

Most are familiar with the concept of Peak Oil, the point at which we reach the maximum rate of petroleum extraction globally. The investment industry may be experiencing a peak of its own, in this case the point of the maximum rate at which it extracts value from its clients' assets. Let's call it Peak Gravy.

If such a peak is indeed reached and the investment industry sees its profits fall, we would regard it as unambiguously good. Such a comment may sound odd coming from a fund manager, but we have never held the wider investment industry in high regard. It seems to us that most funds' fees are too high, most so-called investors' time-horizons are too short, and most firms focus on their own interests rather than on their clients'.

The financial industry itself creates little of value. It is a facilitator, a lubricant for the economy, helping savers to earn a good return on their money and providing financing for investment opportunities, from the funding of a new car to the construction of a spaceship. Those of us who work within it should be humble about the role we play. Rather than "masters of the universe", financiers should aspire to the sort of role in society described by John Maynard Keynes in his 1930 article, *Economic Possibilities for our Grandchildren*: "If economists could manage to get themselves thought of as humble, competent people, on a level with dentists, that would be splendid!"

That investment managers haven't yet managed to reach the level of dentists has several causes. One is that investment strategies are to some degree seen as Veblen Goods – the higher the price, the better the quality – even though studies suggest this not to be the case. In addition, fees are typically struck relative to the level of assets under management. So while firms trying to win business will take risks, holding out promises of differentiation and genuinely active management in order to attract clients, once those clients have been won, the manager's emphasis shifts to protecting what they have in order to hold on to the assets for as long as possible. The simplest way to do this is to avoid taking risk by staying close to the index. While doing so may minimise the likelihood of poor relative returns, it also, of course, minimises the likelihood of good ones, condemning many clients to expensive mediocrity in their investment results.

How high should fees be?

Perversely, the current structure of investment management fees leaves the manager's reward guaranteed, at least for a period of time, and the client bearing the risk of an uncertain outcome. The rule of thumb seems to be that asset managers should reasonably share around a quarter of the gross value added above the benchmark return. In the isolated case of an individual firm managing to add value over the long term, that doesn't seem excessive. But there is a fallacy of composition here: an approach that appropriately rewards one successful investment firm means at the same time that the active management industry in aggregate delivers returns after fees that fall short of the benchmark return.

The industry should, in my view, evolve to a model based on a low base fee, sufficient to cover costs so that an asset management firm can continue to invest during the inevitable periods when its results are poor, combined with a sliding, and capped, performance fee. The base fee might, for instance, be 20 basis points, and the performance capture a fifth of the total above 1 percent. Instead of the hedge fund industry's infamous 'two-and-twenty' (an annual fee of 2 percent of assets under management, plus 20 percent of profits above a certain benchmark), we would end up with something closer to 'point-two-and-twenty', striking a far better balance between the interests of client and manager.

The costs that clients pay matter hugely of course, but only in the context of total returns – as in so much else, we need to make a clear distinction between price and value. At present, the investment industry in aggregate does a poor job and does it expensively; no wonder our clients' focus has shifted largely to price. Like the US grocery industry in the 1960s when Sam Walton started Wal-Mart, there are too many people charging too much. There is a large pool of investors that just wants simple products at a low price, and they should seek out the investment equivalent of Wal-Mart. And there is a part of the market that is willing to pay slightly more for a significantly better product. Genuinely differentiated investment strategies that deliver long-term value for their clients should not be sold at discount-store prices.

What should the investment management industry look like?

It should be smaller. There are currently too many spoons in the bowl, too many managers extracting rent from the assets belonging to long-term savers. As in any other industry, firms offering me-too products or failing to add value for their clients should go out of business.

There should be a decent proportion of assets allocated to passive managers, who offer a low-cost benchmark for the active industry to beat. But the whole industry can't go this way: at one level passive investing isn't really investing at all, it's buying cheap market access.

The industry should bear more of its own costs – and those costs should increase as it invests more in in-house corporate governance and investment research functions. Combined with lower fees this means it should become less profitable. The foot-dragging attempts by many asset managers to avoid paying for broker research themselves under the EU's Markets in Financial Instruments Directive (MiFID II) shone an unflattering light on their approach to these things.

It should encourage positive behaviour at the companies in which it invests. The investment industry has explicit costs, but it also has hidden ones from the corporate behaviours that it incentivises. And these hidden costs may be even more damaging to society. The most damaging of these behaviours are short-termism, a fear of uncertainty, and a narrow focus on shareholder value. By acting as if the next quarter is more important than the next decade, the investment industry discourages companies from investing for long-term value creation. By emphasising shareholder value ahead of the interests of all stakeholders, companies risk losing their social licence to operate. This is not how capitalism is supposed to work.

And a plea in the opposite direction: if our societies are to continue shifting the responsibility for savings onto individuals, those individuals must be educated about the decisions they are taking and make sense of the deluge of information that at present serves only to confuse, not enlighten. Perhaps simple, clear investor education should be our next endeavour.

Logic dictates that alongside the greater emphasis on the way listed companies are governed we need to ask, 'Who guards the guards?', and scrutinise the governance, culture and motivations of investment firms themselves. The relationship between an investment manager and its client should be genuinely symbiotic; that it is currently seen as more parasitic in nature is a challenge our industry itself needs to address.

17. Productive bubbles

William Janeway

Not all bubbles are alike. The credit bubble of 2005-08 leading to the global financial crisis was radically unproductive. A mountain of leverage was built on a tiny amount of capital, so when asset prices declined slightly, the collapse in credit was extreme and starved the real economy of working capital. On the other hand, the 1990s dotcom bubble not only funded the building of the infrastructure of the internet, it also funded the first great wave of exploration of what to do with this infrastructure. When this bubble burst, the economic consequences were limited and contained within the scope of conventional policy. The critical factor was the relative lack of leverage by public market investors buying tradable securities.

Asset prices are backward looking and tell you something about what's going on. They are also forward looking because they're an inducement to action. The response to the price signal changes the signal, what George Soros calls reflexivity. That is fundamental in the financial market. But it leads to locally rational behaviour producing an incoherent systemic breakdown. The signature of a bubble is that the demand curve inverts and instead of demand declining as prices rise, demand increases.

Finance theory tells you that there is a fundamental value of every share, the expected net present value of the future cash flows. But as prices move, the arbitragers, the investors who are supposed to rationally know what that fundamental value is, don't dare sell shares that are rising too high or buy shares that are falling too low because if they do it too soon, they're behind the market. Then their investors will take their money away. Up until the 1960s, stock prices were twice as volatile as the underlying cash flows of American business. Since 1990, they have become six to ten times more volatile. The people managing other people's money can afford to be wrong for a shorter and shorter time.

These volatile valuations in the market play a critical role in governing the flow of investment into the real economy. It's a game where speculators and entrepreneurs respond to each other's signals. The entrepreneur sees the speculator bid the price up and concludes that the speculator knows something about the future to take advantage of. Capital is becoming cheaper, so the entrepreneur invests. The speculators see that, think the entrepreneur knows more about the market than they do, and try to get in on the business. So the game goes back and forth, and is likely to be played more intensely during periods of intense technological or institutional change. Really risky start-ups may require a bubble to get funded at all, because only then are investors likely to believe that they can get a return even if it's by selling shares to others before they have to find out whether the company is worth anything.

The bubble, by creating an environment in which risk-taking is rational, solves a co-ordination failure. If I'm invited to be the first round investor in your start-up and I know that you only want five-million pounds now but you're going to need 25 million pounds to have a hope of getting a positive cash flow, how do I know there's going to be the next 20 million or even the next 5 million behind me? In a bubble you stop worrying about whether there is going to be more money behind you. The co-ordination failure through time is eliminated. That is the functional role that bubbles can play at the frontier of the innovation economy. Some bets will fail, others will pay off. Most start-ups that were founded during the dotcom bubble at the end of the 1990s failed completely, but those that succeeded, succeeded very well.

This has been the case historically, too. Every decade from 1825 to the First World War saw some kind of maniacal bubble on the London Stock Exchange. These financed what would turn out to be highly productive core innovations such as the railways, but then London seemed to become vaccinated against speculating on risky new technologies. This may be why leadership in the innovation economy passed to the United States. Although most of new auto firms launched on the New York exchange soon went bust, some went on to become giants, just as PC firms would nearly a century later. Electrification is another illustration. During the 1920s, the mobilisation of capital overcoming that co-ordination failure led to massive investment in electrification in the United States. Electrification is an extreme example of the challenges to rational investors. It needs enormous capital just to produce anything, a flow of electrons. The marginal cost of the incremental electron is zero, similar to the incremental bit being moved across the internet.

If you have competitive conditions and prices move to marginal costs, the player with the most money wins because everybody else goes bankrupt along the way. They can't service the debt incurred to build the generating plant or the distribution network to deliver a service whose marginal cost approaches zero. However, in a bubble, the first movers will win and during the 1920s, the hottest stocks were the new electricity companies. Before the frenzy ended 13 to 33 million kilowatts were installed and delivering electricity across the country, the way the internet now delivers bits.

The killer app of electrification in the home was radio. This leads us to the often-ignored role of the government in building platforms. The United States Navy and the Department of Commerce assembled all of the patents to fight what appeared to be British dominance through the Marconi patents and produced an American company, RCA, capable of winning. RCA became the dominant technological player over the course of 60 years, first for radio and then for television.

Billions of government dollars also played a major role in the great wave of innovation that started in the early 1960s. If you took money from the government, you had to license your patents even to your fiercest competitors at a fair and reasonable price. If you sold something to the Defense Department that mattered, you had to put a competitor into production. This was how national security trumped conventional economics, and arguably accelerated the computer revolution by a generation and created a reservoir of accessible technology available to entrepreneurs and the venture capitalists who backed them.

Even when they burst, productive bubbles leave a useful legacy. The infrastructure for e-commerce and rail transport still serve us.

Sources

NAEC seminar "Doing Capitalism in the Innovation Economy", OECD, 24 May 2018
http://www.oecd.org/naec/events/doing-capitalism-in-the-innovation-economy.htm

NAEC seminar "Productive bubbles", OECD, 8 February 2016,
http://www.oecd.org/naec/events/productive-bubbles.htm

18. Aligning the financial system with sustainable development

Simon Zadek

Financing the Sustainable Development Goals (SDGs) and the Paris Agreement commitments on climate requires trillions of dollars per year. Much of the finance needed will have to come from private sources, yet inadequate private capital is being deployed in ways that are aligned to these goals and commitments. Ample evidence exists that the financial system is out of step with its core purpose of ensuring that finance flows support the long-term needs of balanced, sustained growth. Policy and market failures were spectacularly in evidence as drivers of the financial crisis in 2008.

The *Inquiry into the Design of a Sustainable Financial System* was initiated by the UN Environment Programme in 2014, and completed its mandate in 2018, but many of its work streams will continue in other forms. The Inquiry aimed to shape a narrative that demonstrated the need for system change in finance in pursuit of sustainable development, echoing the experience coming from many countries, market actors and collaborative platforms. It looked at how to address policy and market failures and turn the global financial system around to deliver the financing needed to transition to sustainable development. It focused on the 'rules of the game' governing financial and capital markets, and therefore the roles of central banks, financial regulators and standard-setters, stock exchanges and the like.

In 2014, a sustainable financial system meant focusing on resilience to financial crisis rather than capital allocation aligned to wider environmental, social and economic goals. Now, a sustainable financial system has a more profound meaning –a financial system that serves the transition to sustainable development. Sustainability is becoming part of the routine practice within financial institutions and regulatory bodies. A growing number of commitments to action are being made, matched by the beginnings of the reallocation of capital.

Some take-off has happened in areas such as investment in renewable energy, green bonds, fiduciary duty and risk-based disclosure. But substantial lags remain in large parts of the system, for example, in housing finance, often the largest asset class in banking portfolios, and infrastructure investments. There has been a fourteen-fold increase in labelled green bond issuance from USD 11 billion in 2013 to USD 155 billion in 2017. Key to this growth has been the market-creating role of public authorities, including key development banks. Such progress needs to be set against the scale of the global bond market of around USD 100 trillion. On the other hand, divestments in carbon-intensive assets reached an estimated USD 5 trillion in 2016, versus around USD 710 billion investments in coal, oil and gas.

National action is critical, but some national plans catalyse, broader international action. For example, China's "Guidelines for Establishing a Green Financial System" are the world's most comprehensive set of national commitments, covering priorities across banking, capital markets and insurance; and the EU High-Level Expert Group on Sustainable Finance has laid the foundations for a comprehensive action plan on sustainable finance. The global number and range of policy measures to advance aspects of sustainable finance has increased. At the end of 2013, 139 subnational, national-level and international policy and regulatory measures were in place across 44 jurisdictions. Most of these were first-generation efforts to improve disclosure in securities markets and by pension funds. Four years on, the number of measures has not only doubled – to 300 in 54 jurisdictions – but the pattern of activity has changed, with a substantial rise in system-level initiatives, which now account for a quarter of the total.

There has been a striking growth in international initiatives to share experience, stimulate action and promote co-operation on key rules and standards, such as the recent formation of a network of some of the world's leading central banks to contribute to fighting climate change. Other structurally significant initiatives include the Financial Stability Board's private sector-led Task Force on Climate-related Financial

Disclosures (TCFD) as an industry-led initiative to draw up voluntary guidance on reporting by business and financial institutions.

National priorities as a starting point for a wider wave of changes is more effective than blueprinting change in a more formulaic manner. For example, building a digital infrastructure for greater financial inclusion in Kenya has also enabled the more effective deployment of clean energy and improved access to health services. While the Inquiry focused on countries with larger, evolving financial systems, especially emerging markets, because of their desire to influence traditional international rule-setting institutions in pursuit of national development priorities, countries with only modest financial systems can be influential by virtue of their willingness to innovate beyond the norm.

Some capital is flowing to the new economy, but far more is supporting the old economy, through an inability or unwillingness on the part of owners and intermediaries to redeploy it. The next phase in sustainable finance will be about making the shift from acknowledgement to alignment. It will be multidimensional and non-linear. It will involve mainstreaming but also replacing the mainstream by new, better ways of doing finance. It will encompass a sense of purpose for the financial system matched by a decentralised model of delivery. All this will mean new performance metrics that measure the extent to which sustainability is really part of the process of finance as well as its outcomes.

The Inquiry's work with the World Bank Group in producing the 'Roadmap for a Sustainable Financial System' enabled it to identify developments needed to accelerate the flow of sustainable finance. Some actions can be taken by market actors, such as disclosure, but even these may need policy or regulatory interventions to advance at scale and speed. Other measures require policy interventions in the broadest sense, which would include a combination of policy, regulatory, standard-setting, judicial and fiscal actions, often working in concert with, and supportive of, market innovations and broader developments. The Inquiry has helped to link the financial system with sustainable development. The evidence indicates the potential for a strong next wave of action.

Sources

NAEC Seminar "Inquiry into the design of a sustainable finance system", OECD, 30 September 2015, http://www.oecd.org/naec/events/inquiry-into-the-design-of-a-sustainable-financial-system.htm

"Making Waves: Aligning the Financial System with Sustainable Development", UNEP, 2018 http://unepinquiry.org/making-waves/

19. Inequality and rent-seeking in the finance sector

Angus Deaton

We should be careful not to confuse inequality with unfairness. It is the perception of unfairness that is driving populism, while some kinds of inequality seem acceptable. For example rags-to-riches stories seem to confirm that the American Dream can become a reality, even if the rising net worth and access to privilege of the person who succeeds contribute to inequality. To understand inequality, we have to consider the economy as a set of processes and policies whose interactions produce various outcomes, including inequality. Some of these processes are good, some are bad, and only by sorting the good from the bad can we understand inequality and what to do about it.

History shows that some societies with little or no inequality had little or no economic growth either, and it is possible to find examples of various combinations of high/low growth/inequality. In *The Great Escape: Health, Wealth, and the Origins of Inequality*, I show that periods of great progress are usually periods of rising inequality. So rising inequality can be a sign of real progress, but that is not what is happening now.

One of the main causes of rising inequality today is rent-seeking. Mancur Olson said that this is what would happen in mature capitalism, and you could make an argument that this has been happening all along except for a brief period when the Second World War stopped it for a while. If monopolies are unregulated, they can be very effective at squeezing profits out of consumers and workers. That's a process of rent-seeking which would transfer resources upwards, from relatively-poor people to people who are much better-off, thus increasing inequality but also slowing economic growth and making the market less efficient. Under those circumstances you would get a correlation between inequality and slower growth, but it is the monopolies that are causing both, not one causing the other.

Rent-seeking does not have to redistribute upwards—when there were powerful unions, there was a fair amount of redistributing downward, to autoworkers in Detroit for example when there was little competition. Now big companies are not sharing the rents with the workers anymore and one of the reasons people are worried about inequality is that rent-seeking is now almost entirely in favour of the elite.

As a consequence, the living standards of the working class are not rising anymore. This is not just an economics issue. We are seeing "deaths of despair" from drugs, alcohol and suicide that Anne Case and I have been analysing - people dying in middle age. In Mortality and morbidity in the 21st century, we find that while midlife mortality rates continue to fall among all education classes in most of the rich world, middle-aged non-Hispanic whites in the United States with a high school diploma or less have experienced increasing midlife mortality since the late 1990s. This is due to both rises in the number of deaths of despair and to a slowdown in progress against mortality from heart disease and cancer, the two largest killers in middle age. The combined effect means that mortality rates of whites with no more than a high school degree, which were around 30 percent lower than mortality rates of blacks in 1999, grew to be 30 percent higher than blacks by 2015.

The increases in deaths of despair are accompanied by a measurable deterioration in economic and social wellbeing, which has become more pronounced for each successive birth cohort. Marriage rates, labour force participation rates, and other indicators linked to well-being such as various forms of social participation, fall between successive birth cohorts, while reports of physical pain, and poor health and mental health rise.

Some aspects of globalisation and technological change, like outsourcing and robotics, also suppress worker wages while benefiting the rich. But these alone cannot explain why median incomes have stagnated for half a century, while incomes at the top have grown. The answer lies in a series of unfair economic and social processes that propagate inequality.

Healthcare financing. Each year, the United States spends a trillion dollars (USD 8000 per family) more than other wealthy nations on healthcare costs, with worse outcomes. Healthcare jobs grew the second fastest in 2017, but wages were largely flat, leading hospital workers to unionise for higher pay. Healthcare financing cuts wages for the average American too - most employer-sponsored healthcare benefits are actually taken out workers' pay rather than being paid for by the company.

Mergers. Many industries, like tech, media, and healthcare, are now run by a few, large companies. But mergers rarely boost the wages of workers. Because of hospital mergers, hospital prices have risen, while hospital wages have not. Big companies have an easier time manipulating public policy to accrue profits, instead of making money through innovation and investment.

Low federal minimum wage. The federal minimum wage, at USD 7.25 an hour, has changed since 2009. According to a 2017 YouGov Survey, 66 percent of US adults would like to see the minimum wage raised to USD 10.10. But the policy change usually faces resistance in Congress, where wealthy firms exert disproportionate influence.

Diminishing worker power. Twenty percent of workers sign non-compete clauses. This used to be restricted to employees with access to exclusive information or expertise, but now even blue-collar workers doing low-skill service jobs are being asked to sign, thereby reducing their incomes and bargaining power by preventing them from taking on other work. This is in fact is illegal but the law is not enforced. What's more, over half of non-union, privately employed Americans - some 60 million people - have signed mandatory arbitration agreements, which means they can never sue their employers.

The rise of temporary contracts. Companies are increasingly replacing full-time, salaried workers with contractors. Janitors, servers, and maintenance staff who once worked for wealthy companies now work for independent service corporations that compete aggressively against each other over pricing. Working conditions are precarious, without benefits, and with little opportunity for promotion.

The stock market. While the stock market rewards innovation, it also incentivises companies to shuffle resources from labour to capital. As median wages have stagnated, corporate profits relative to GDP have grown 20 percent to 25 percent. That number would be even higher if executive pay was tracked as profits instead of salaries.

Corporate influence on politics. Both the Consumer Financial Protection Bureau and the 2010 Dodd-Frank legislation are under attack. President Trump plans to attack 75 percent of regulations, and may roll back a rule that requires money managers to prioritise their clients' interests. The US Supreme Court has ruled that corporations can act as political entities, spending unlimited amounts to support candidates and the legislation they will eventually push.

Source

NAEC seminar with Angus Deaton, OECD, 16 May 2018
https://www.oecd.org/naec/events/why-is-global-poverty-so-hard-to-measure-and-to-eradicate.htm

20. Currency: Between debt and sovereignty

Michel Aglietta

The concept of money implies a profound reversal of the way the economy is represented. Neoclassical economists postulate a generic individual, with a specific property, utility, that does not depend on the utility of others. Utilities are exogenous. The market is the exclusive mode of co-ordination and this makes it possible to define an intellectual project that is ideological: a discipline independent of the social, whereas in reality economic and other human activities are integrated by a link with the collective we can call society. If society is your starting point, the relationship of the individual to the collective is fundamental. Money is the concept that expresses this generic relationship in the economic order. It is a specific language, a language of numbers. A language gives meaning to others. The meaning for others determined by money is what will be called value. Money and value are intrinsically linked. The functions of money will come as a characteristic of the process by which value is determined, because value is determined only by the generic relationship of economic actors to money, that is, payment. The generic process of co-ordinating a society in which individuals exchange objects in the form of value must be determined.

We do not need a metaphor to define co-ordination. Co-ordination is objective, and observable: it is the payments system. Money as an institution produces rules for the issue of means of payment, rules for clearing and settlement from which an overall co-ordination of exchanges takes place. The payment system is an institution and cannot be appropriated, but it must be guided by policy, so money is essentially political.

In the history of money, there has been a debate going on for centuries formalised in the opposition between the currency principle and banking principle. The opposition centres on two characteristics: endogenous and exogenous money.

The orthodox view is based on an exogenous hypothesis of external money or money as a specific commodity defined only by quantity. Market exchange co-ordination occurs through market discovery mechanisms (and not through the payment system). The real demand for money is derived from the theory of utility value: real wealth and opportunity cost. In market equilibrium money is neutral: it doesn't impinge upon equilibrium real prices. Money equilibrium determines only its own price.

According to the alternative, endogenous hypothesis of internal money, or money entirely related to the credit system, money is created as the counterpart of debt. The trade of debt is a trade of promises which can be plagued by uncertainty. Money is the fundamental institution (a way that we encompass a social contract within society). The payment system precedes the trade, clearing and settlement of debt. The finality of payment through the settlement mechanism of all daily payments ratifies the exchanges that have ratified value.

So, for the exogenous hypothesis, value is absolute and logically precedes the function of money, while in the endogenous hypothesis value is relative and is a pure social relationship. The value of money logically precedes the value of goods.

Endogenous money cannot be neutral, by nature. The link between exogeneity and neutrality of money is intrinsic. Hence the strong opposition between these two characteristics. In a concept of neutral money the bank is not a creator of money. It is only a transmission belt of the central bank, resulting in a monetary multiplier (a function of the interest rate), itself modulated by the behaviour of money seekers. In this exogenous conception of money creation, under the assumption that the demand for money is a stable function, Friedman can claim that inflation is always and everywhere a monetary phenomenon, caused by the public authority in charge of monetary creation. The 2008 financial crisis and its aftermath proved otherwise. Central banks created huge amounts of money (in the order of USD 10 trillion). If the currency were neutral, there would have been hyperinflation because the supply of money would have been in enormous excess of stable demand. If you offer a huge amount of money that nobody wants, you create inflation. In fact, the problem has been to avoid deflation. Reality refuted the monetarists' hypothesis.

As well as being an institution and a language, money has something that makes it ambivalent, that makes it appropriable. Liquidity is appropriable and therefore exchangeable. In this form, the value appears condensed, and disconnected from the public institution that is the payments system. Liquidity means you can make money with money. Through liquidity, money becomes the social form of wealth. Any particular wealth is only reflected in the amount of liquidity to which it could be equivalent. Contrary to the neoclassical conception, money is demanded because others demand it. This externality of demand violates the rule that prices are related purely to the desires of the individual independently of others.

When we look at the international financial system, we see that there is a global economy but no global currency. If capital did not circulate, there would be no problem since capital controls would maintain separate currencies. But with globalisation, an organisation is needed. In the nineteenth century, the gold standard was a way of tackling the question of an international currency, even if the convertibility of gold remained under the control of nations. The Bretton Woods system after the Second World War was an international institutionalised monetary system that established the preponderance of the dollar, as part of a set of common rules and procedures administered by an international institution, the IMF. Capital controls allowed this international arrangement to function because it preserved sufficient monetary autonomy for nations. The collapse of the Bretton Woods system removed international monetary rules. Monetary relations become directly dependent on exchange of liquidity on foreign exchange markets, and thus on unstable private arbitrage, which is reflected in exchange rate fluctuations.

Why elect one currency over another, a national currency that other nations will accept? The answer lies in the realm of hegemony and geopolitics.

Sources

NAEC seminar "Currency: between debt and sovereignty", OECD, 18 May 2016
http://www.oecd.org/naec/events/currency-between-debt-and-sovereignty.htm

La Monnaie entre dettes et souveraineté, Michel Aglietta, Pepita Ould Ahmed, Jean-François Ponsot, Éditions Odile Jacob, 2016 https://www.odilejacob.fr/catalogue/sciences-humaines/economie-et-finance/monnaie-entre-dettes-et-souverainete_9782738133830.php

Entretien avec Michel Aglietta, Adrien Faudot, Revue Interventions économiques, 59, 2017
http://journals.openedition.org/interventionseconomiques/3958

21. Insurance: can systemic risk get any more systemic post Covid-19?

Edite Ligere

One of the roles of the insurance sector is to contribute to financial stability by enabling natural and legal persons to take risks they otherwise may not be able or willing to take. Insuring against business interruption is one example of cover offered by insurance providers, as well as Lloyd's of London, the oldest insurance market in the world. Founded around 1686, Lloyd's has weathered losses arising from triggers varying from earthquakes to terrorist attacks, yet it has never been faced with so many business interruption claims on a global scale simultaneously as now.

The societal and economic impact of Covid-19 is testing the capacity of the global insurance sector in an unprecedented way. This could lead to higher capital requirements for insurers, much higher premiums, the widening of risks excluded from insurance cover, tighter limits on insurance cover, or perhaps an increasing reluctance to underwrite certain risks. It could also lead to changes in how the industry is regulated and governed.

The Financial Stability Board (FSB) was created after the 2008 financial crisis to co-ordinate the work of national financial regulatory authorities; develop and promote the implementation of effective regulatory, supervisory and other financial sector policies under the auspices of the G20 and on the recommendation of standard setting bodies such as the International Association of Insurance Supervisors, and the Basel Committee of Banking Supervision. The FSB's decisions do not have force in international law. It is a member driven organisation which forms judgments of risks to financial stability. Where possible, it agrees international standards or approaches to policy. National authorities ultimately decide whether and how to implement such standards.

While the FSB is a process more than an institution, it is important to appreciate the practical significance of the political comity (mutual recognition) which generally exists among members. Considerations of comity contribute to the evolution of views and approaches to financial regulation among national supervisors; and to the likelihood that national supervisors will act according to the recommendations of the FSB. Such political comity is likely to make the work of the FSB increasingly relevant to identifying and mitigating systemic risks to the global economy.

Unlike many other countries, insurance in the United States is regulated on a State rather than a federal level. The National Association of Insurance Commissioners, established in1871, provides a forum for State insurance regulators to co-ordinate their activities. The Financial Stability Oversight Council's (FSOC) mandate under the 2010 Dodd-Frank Act includes identification of systemic risks; promoting market discipline; and responding to emerging threats to the financial stability of the United States. Systemic risk is defined as "a risk of an event or development that could impair financial intermediation or financial market functioning to a degree that would be sufficient to inflict significant damage on the broader economy".

Apart from monitoring the financial services marketplace to identify potential threats to US financial stability, FSOC's duties include recommending to its member agencies general supervisory priorities and principles; recommending to primary financial regulatory agencies to apply new or heightened standards and safeguards for financial activities or practices that could create or increase risks of significant liquidity, credit, or other problems spreading among financial companies and markets; and designating non-bank financial companies for supervision and regulation by the Federal Reserve, including the application of prudential standards.

There are fundamental differences in the business models and balance sheets of banks. For example, the long-term nature of some insurance liabilities and the consequent risks to the global economy posed by such liabilities are different from the much shorter-term liabilities of banking institutions and the greater risks such liabilities pose to the wider economy. The 2008 financial crisis was mainly caused by systemic risks in the banking sector rather than traditional insurance activities.

In July 2013, FSOC designated AIG and GE Capital as the first non-bank SIFIs – systemically important financial institutions. Prudential was designated in September 2013 and MetLife in December 2014. All three US non-bank SIFIs have since been de-designated. In 2017, President Trump directed the Secretary of the Treasury, who chairs FSOC, to review the non-bank SIFI designation process and make recommendations for regulatory or legislative changes to the process. The Treasury's report concluded that FSOC should focus more on identifying systemically risky activities than on designating individual firms; consult with regulators of companies engaging in such activities to address systemic risk; and designate individual companies only as a last resort. The activities-based approach to the identification and mitigation of systemic risk is intended to enable FSOC to identify and address potential risks and emerging threats on a system-wide basis and "reduce the potential for competitive market distortions" that could arise from designating specific entities.

Products, activities, or practices to be reviewed include those related to the extension of credit; the use of leverage or short-term funding; the provision of guarantees of financial performance; and other key functions critical to support the operation of financial markets. Examples of markets FSOC would monitor include corporate and sovereign debt and loans; equity; markets for other financial products, including structured products and derivatives; short-term funding markets; payment, clearing, and settlement functions; new or evolving financial products, activities, and practices; and developments affecting the resiliency of financial market participants. If FSOC identified a product, activity, or practice that could pose a systemic risk, it would consult with relevant financial regulatory agencies to determine whether the potential risk merited further review or action.

The ambitious aim post-2008 was to create a global regulatory level playing field for the "too big to fail" and other global financial institutions. Will one of the objectives of the post-Covid-19 regulatory effort be to attempt to reverse some of the consequences of globalisation? In a systemic crisis such as Covid-19, the nation state is still the ultimate arbiter and protector of the fate of its citizens and others within its territory. In the context of global financial groups operating across multiple jurisdictions, the development of a harmonised, legally enforceable framework for the identification and mitigation of systemic risk is a Herculean task. While there continues to be increasing discussion among supervisory authorities and broad political consensus in respect of the shape of the principles regarded as conducive to global financial stability, the legal implementation and enforcement of such principles remains the responsibility of national authorities. But for how long?

22. Lessons from the financial crisis

John Llewellyn

There was no single cause of the 2007-2008 crisis. The crisis was systemic, with fear and greed interacting with the prevailing macroeconomic conditions, macroeconomic policies, and the regulatory framework to break down both confidence and trust. The abolition of the US Glass-Steagall Act did however play a major part. That Act separated commercial and investment banking to eliminate conflicts of interest that arise, as they did in the 1930s, when the granting of credit – lending – and the use of credit – investing – were undertaken by a single institution. With the abolition of Glass-Steagall, the stage was set for these conflicts to come back.

Equally important, however, were the ways in which behaviour unfolded. Savers, seeking yield, were relaxed about moving into assets that historically had been risky. US investment banks borrowed extensively on the wholesale money market, lending massively to households through mortgages and loans, further fuelling the property boom. Mortgage mis-selling aided the process, with sellers being paid per sale, while bearing no responsibility for the consequences. Investment banks invented complex, highly geared investment vehicles, many of which they funded on the wholesale money market and then sold on to other parties so that they did not appear on the banks' balance sheets. The explosion of leverage was boosted by the 'shadow banking' world of hedge funds, private equity firms, and other unregulated financial companies, the demand side of the trade in collateralised debt obligations (CDOs), mortgage-backed securities, credit default swaps (CDSs), and the like.

When asset values turned, confidence and trust collapsed and leverage, which had been everybody's friend, turned into a savage enemy. Various factors explain why so few people realised what was happening, or acted to stop it.

Incentive structures encouraged traders to make unwarrantedly risky bets, but all traders have individual risk limits and banks' managements set those limits.

Poor corporate risk analysis. Within the investment banks, some risk managers were concerned that the risk models did not adequately take underlying macroeconomic risks into account. Many senior risk managers were reluctant to admit that they did not really understand their banks' risk models. And most managements did not appreciate that sponsors would not be able to avoid responsibility for their supposedly off-balance-sheet products.

Undue reliance on Value at Risk (VAR) analysis. This statistical technique has two serious limitations: information at the extremities – where catastrophic risk lies – was sparse, particularly after 15 years of exceptionally low macro volatility; accommodating framework conditions that evolve requires a structural framework, which a statistical distribution alone does not provide. Sometimes the model simply may not describe reality at all.

Unwillingness of corporate management to act.

Poor corporate governance. Boards of Directors proved too weak, or too ill-informed, to challenge 'successful' CEOs. Managements appear increasingly to have run companies for themselves, and shareholders proved unwilling or unable to rein management back.

'Grade inflation' by the credit rating agencies implied, for example, that a mortgage vehicle rated as 'triple A' carried the same risk as similarly-rated major-country government bonds. CRAs became conflicted, accepting fees for certifying that the new vehicles were high grade. At root, the CRAs' business model contains an unresolvable conflict: the people who pay for their services are not those who use them.

Regulatory Authorities did a poor job. They relied too heavily on companies "doing the right thing", with too few checks; and they failed to achieve the basic separation of risk from reward; and financial regulation from financial activity.

Capital ratios proved to be inadequate, given the leverage the SEC permitted. The total amount the financial sector wrote off after August 2007 was over 100 times its collective VAR assessment of 18 months previously.

The pro-cyclical impact of "mark-to-market" valuation techniques exacerbated the capital inadequacy of banks. When crashing "fire-sale" values are used by auditors to value a bank's assets, they induce fire sales to spread, thereby deepening the crisis.

A deficient understanding of corporate self-interest led regulators to believe that managements would always have their company's survival as their primary objective, and so would avoid actions that would unduly jeopardise survival. This faith however underestimates management's personal short-term objectives; the unawareness of many CEOs of the scale of the risks of macroeconomic origin to which they were exposed; and the degree to which competitive pressures obliged each to do broadly what all the others were doing.

International organisations failed to press the point. The Bank for International Settlements sounded alarm bells and the IMF and the European Central Bank expressed concern, but in the policy world as a whole, much as in the investment banks, no one wanted to hear.

A number of broad policy proposals might have reduced the likelihood, or at least the severity, of the crisis. (Whether they would help with the next crisis, however, which will be different, is another matter.)

Macroeconomic policy:

- Pay greater attention to imbalances.

- Direct policy at any major macroeconomic variable that departs significantly from any historical relationship.

- Agree a better method of identifying bubbles. Minsky, for example, identified bubbles as any occasion when large numbers start trading in markets they don't understand.

Regulatory policy:

- Require the Regulatory Authorities to report on the potential financial sector implications of macroeconomic imbalances.

- Establish ex ante the conditions whereby it is appropriate to take over a distressed bank, ideally when its net worth is still positive, so that it can continue as a going concern.

- Raise capital adequacy ratios, at least for any bank that operates with its deposits guaranteed.

- Require banks to operate a pro-cyclical reserves policy.

- Oblige the CRAs to recover from their conflicted failure. There may be a case for two types of credit rating agency, one to carry out legislated supervisory responsibilities, the second undertaken for business for profit but with no role in supervision.

- Discourage off-balance-sheet activities and put the onus on the proposer to explain why they are in the public interest.

We often hear that "nobody saw it coming", but there were pointers. At Lehman Brothers we had a tool called Damocles for predicting financial crises in developing countries. A Damocles reading above 75 implied a one-in-three chance of a financial crisis over the coming 12 months, and a reading above 100 implied a 50-50 chance. Almost as a joke at first, we also ran the United States through the model. We concluded that while G10 economies can "get away with" poorer scores, and for longer, than emerging market economies, the US score had been between 75 and 100 over the 10 years before the crisis. Moreover, the United States ranked second, between Iceland (worst) and Romania (third). The main negative signals were coming from external debt, the current account, and credit.

Source

NAEC Conference "10 Years after the failure of Lehman Brothers: What have we learned?", OECD, 13-14 September 2018, http://www.oecd.org/naec/10-years-after-the-crisis/

3 Financial Policy

This section assesses what lessons have been learned from the financial crisis and what has changed in the financial system and its relation to the rest of the economy since 2008, and considers how the financial system stood up to the pressures of the Covid-19 pandemic. It retraces the road taken from the Bretton Woods agreements to the bailouts of the banking system in 2008. It examines the role of prudential regulation in managing the financial system, and debates whether evolution or revolution is needed for macro stabilisation. It discusses the equity aspects of regulatory reform. The section also analyses the role of monetary finance in dealing with debt. It examines new financial vulnerabilities and suggests ways policymakers might deal with them.

23. From Bretton Woods to bailouts

Yanis Varoufakis

The most common explanations of the 2008 crisis (growing trade imbalances, financialisation, etc.) are themselves symptoms of an underlying global macro dynamic that has been unfolding since the 1940s: the transformation of the United States from an hegemonic economy whose surplus was used to stabilise Europe and Japan, to a deficit economy whose hegemony grew as a result of stabilising global aggregate demand via its growing twin deficits. To see this, we need to go back to the 1944 Bretton Woods Conference. The US administration understood that the only way of avoiding a post-war depression was to recycle America's surpluses to Europe and Japan, and thus generate abroad the demand that would be met by American factories when the war ended.

The result was the project of dollarising Europe, founding the European Union as a cartel of heavy industry, and building up Japan, within a global currency union (the Bretton Woods system) and its underlying philosophy whereby money was co-owned by those who had it and the global community that backed it. The system featured fixed exchange rates anchored to the dollar, almost constant interest rates, banks operating under severe capital controls, and American-led management of global aggregate demand. This brought the United States a Golden Age of low unemployment, low inflation, high growth, and diminished inequality.

In the late 1960s however, the foundation of Bretton Woods was disintegrating. By 1968, America had lost its surpluses, slipped into a burgeoning twin deficit and could, therefore, no longer stabilise the global system. This, combined with banks' attempt to free themselves from their constraints, created the offshore, unregulated Eurodollar market that became the basis for financialisation after Bretton Woods was jettisoned on 15 August 1971, when President Nixon announced the ejection of Europe and Japan from the dollar zone.

Washington was unwilling to reduce its deficits by imposing austerity (that would shrink US capacity to project power worldwide), and in fact boosted the deficits. America absorbed exports from Germany, Japan and, later China, ushering in the second phase of post-war growth (1980-2008). Expanding American deficits were financed by around 70 percent of the profits of European, Japanese and Chinese exporters seeking refuge and higher returns. Three developments aided this: lower US wage growth than in Europe and Japan boosting returns to foreign capital; 20 percent+ interest rates; and dollarised financialisation that occasioned self-reinforcing financial paper gains. By the mid-1980s, the United States was absorbing a large portion of global surplus industrial products while Wall Street provided credit to American consumers (whose wages stagnated), channelled direct investment into US corporations; and financed the purchase of US Treasury Bills (i.e. funded American government deficits).

When, after 1991, an additional two billion workers entered the global workforce from China, India and the former Soviet bloc, producing new output that boosted the already imbalanced trade flows, capitalism entered a new phase - globalisation. In globalisation's wake, the EU created its common currency, because, like all cartels, it had to keep the prices of its main oligopolistic industries stable across the single market. To do this, it was necessary to fix exchange rates within its jurisdiction, similar to the Bretton Woods era. However, from 1972 to the early-1990s each EU attempt to fix European exchange rates failed spectacularly. Eventually, the EU decided to establish a single currency, within the supportive (although grossly imbalanced) environment of global stability that the US-anchored global surplus recycling mechanism maintained. To get around the political hurdles presented by the Bundesbank's reluctance to sacrifice the mark, we ended up with the ECB supplying a single currency to the banks of nineteen countries, whose governments would have to salvage these banks during the crisis, without a central bank that could support them.

Meanwhile, Wall Street, and UK, French and German banks were taking advantage of their position in the US-anchored global recycling system to grow on the back of the net profits flowing into the United States. This added energy to the recycling scheme, as it fuelled an ever-accelerating level of demand within the United States, Europe and Asia. It also brought about the decoupling of financial capital flows from the underlying trade flows. To illustrate this, recall Germany's position in August 2007. German net export income from the United States was USD 5 billion. Germany's national accounts registered this surplus as well as a counter-balancing outflow of capital from Germany to the United States. However, the national accounts do not show that from the early 1990s until 2007, German banks were buying into lucrative dollar denominated derivatives with dollars they were borrowing from Wall Street. In August 2007, the price of these derivatives began to fall, underlying debts were going bad, and Wall Street institutions faced large margin calls. German bankers needed dollars in a hurry when their US counterparts began to call in their dollar debts, but no one would buy the toxic derivatives they had purchased. From one moment to the next, German banks swimming in oceans of paper profit found themselves in desperate need of dollars they did not have. Could Germany's bankers not borrow dollars from Germany's exporters to meet their dollar obligations? They could, but how would the USD 5 billion the latter had earned during that August help when the German bankers' outstanding debt to Wall Street the Americans were now calling in exceeded USD 1000 billion?

Politicians intervened to shift the losses away from those who created them. In Europe, the dominant narrative on what went wrong had no basis in macroeconomics and was thus allowed to obscure the reality that the eurosystem had been designed not to have any shock absorbers to absorb the shockwave from Wall Street. Consequently, one nation was turned against another by a political class determined to disguise a crisis caused by an alliance of Northern and Southern bankers and other rent-seeking oligarchs as a clash caused by the profligate Southerners, or as a crisis of over-generous social welfare systems.

While America's trade deficit returned to its pre-crisis levels within a couple of years, it was no longer enough to stabilise global demand. The pre-crisis mechanism which converted the US trade deficit into fixed capital investments around the world has broken down. The Central Banks tried to make amends with QE-induced liquidity. But that only pushed up asset prices in the West, giving US corporations an opportunity to buy back their shares while saving their own profits in offshore accounts. Where monies did flow, in the Emerging Markets, investment grew but was vulnerable both to the deflationary forces from European austerity and to the expectation of tapering and higher long-term interest rates in the United States. Perhaps the only pillar of global demand was China, although its capacity to maintain that boost was circumscribed by the constant threat of its credit bubble bursting.

In short. Wall Street's pre-2008 capacity to continue 'closing' the global recycling loop vanished - and has not been replaced yet. America's banks can no longer harness the United States' twin deficits for the purposes of financing enough demand within America to keep the net exports of the rest of the world going. This is why the world today remains in the grip of the same crisis that began in 2008.

Source

NAEC Conference "10 Years after the failure of Lehman Brothers: What have we learned?", OECD, 13-14 September 2018, http://www.oecd.org/naec/10-years-after-the-crisis/

24. The prudential regulation hypothesis

Erdem Başçı

Long term interest rates are currently at historically low levels in all of the G7 countries. They have tended to fall in both nominal and real terms since early 1980s. Especially after the Global Financial Crisis (GFC) which hit in 2008, interest rates have fallen to zero or even negative levels in many cases. The big question is whether this situation in permanent or temporary. Since nobody knows the answer for sure, a certain degree of prudence is justified as to the pace and the eventual extent of debt accumulation at these very attractive rates.

It is therefore not surprising that after the GFC the prudential standards have been tightened to some extent across the globe. Part of the tightening is the naturally elevated prudence of the private sector to a recently realised risk, part of it is due to tighter prudential standards for microeconomic stability reasons (micro-prudential regulation) or macroeconomic stability reasons (macro-prudential regulation).

In an economic model with one representative consumer, there would be no need to use loan-to-income restriction as a prudential tool, simply because the single consumer would not be demanding any consumer loans whatsoever in equilibrium. The model becomes not only more realistic but also much more interesting once we allow heterogeneity across consumer types. A useful macroeconomic model with a banking sector would need to have at least two types of consumers. One would be the 'patient' type, who lends, the other the 'impatient' type, who borrows. Even in such a simple-looking version, the results become strikingly different from those of a representative consumer model.

The first obvious result from such a model with heterogeneity is that at any point in time, the impatient consumers would find the market interest rate 'too low' and would become borrowers. If there is a banking sector in the model, as debtors they would be placed on the left-hand side of the balance sheets of the banks. The patient part of the population would find the market interest rate 'sufficiently high' and would become lenders. As depositors they would be placed on the right-hand side of the balance sheets.

We could also consider another split, between "I don't know" what the consequences of my financial decision might be, and "I don't care". The former can be dealt with via financial education, while microprudential financial regulation is used to tackle "I don't care."

The presence of prudential regulation can therefore be attributed in part to the existence of heterogeneous behaviour, and the mere existence of prudential regulation points to the need for incorporating heterogeneity into our economic models.

The question then arises of what form this regulation should take. One of the most effectively used macroprudential policy instrument after the financial crisis has been to impose a loan-to-income restriction on consumer loans, for example, a mortgage shouldn't be more than a few times the income, or total monthly debt repayments shouldn't be more than a certain fraction of the income. This makes sense not only for prudential reasons, but also for social sustainability reasons.

Imposing such constraints may exclude potential borrowers from being able to take out additional loans even if interest rates are very low, and even very low levels of real interest rates will not be able to stimulate consumer credit. Yet, the demand for money will continue to grow even at negative interest rates mainly due to transaction demand (money needed for daily transactions) and precautionary demand (keeping some money just in case it might be needed); despite the fact that the demand for money as an asset class will go down sharply. Therefore under the prudential regulation hypothesis (PRH) there is a possibility of sustaining a monetary equilibrium with very low, possibly even negative, interest rates.

Negative real interest rates would not be consistent with attempts other than the PRH to explain the low real interest rates that we currently observe in many countries. Neither the (global) savings glut hypothesis (SGH) of Bernanke, nor the secular stagnation hypothesis (SSH) of Summers would be consistent with negative real rates. The SGH would fail mainly because the subjective interest rate of even the most patient consumer would likely be positive, albeit small. The SSH would fail because the marginal product of capital would remain positive, albeit lower, compared to the past.

If loan-to-income regulation is the most relevant binding constraint for consumer indebtedness, for banks the equivalent is the leverage ratio restriction (LRR) or bank capital requirements. The LRR requires the banks to hold a minimum amount of equity capital as a fraction of their total balance sheet size. This constraint will always be binding as long as bank profitability is sufficiently high. Therefore it will also be a hard constraint on the lending ability of the banking sector, hence their production of money. Macroeconomic models which ignore the effects of LRR on the banking sector will probably overestimate the impacts of monetary and fiscal policies on aggregate demand. The recent stagnant growth of broad money aggregates in all of the G7 countries needs to be studied from this angle.

Before the GFC, both monetary and prudential policies eased gradually over three decades. After the GFC, monetary easing continued but was accompanied with a justifiable degree of tightening in prudential policies. Ten years after the GFC, the big question is whether monetary policy can be normalised and what that 'new normal' would look like, in particular, if negative interest rates would be a permanent feature of the new normal. I argue that they could, together with stagnant growth in broad money aggregates. Even a modest degree of prudential regulation in the financial system may give rise to these two results. In fact a necessary condition for observing negative interest rates in the equilibrium of an economic model is to incorporate prudential regulations as constraints on borrowing. My main message here is that prudential policy matters a lot and should not be ignored by economists.

Source

BIS Papers N° 86: "Macroprudential policy" https://www.bis.org/publ/bppdf/bispap86.pdf

"10 Years after the failure of Lehman Brothers: What have we learned?" NAEC Conference, OECD, 13-14 September 2018, http://www.oecd.org/naec/10-years-after-the-crisis/

25. Rethinking macro stabilisation: Evolution or revolution?

Olivier Blanchard

Before the Great Financial Crisis, macroeconomic paradigms largely ignored the possibility of financial developments as drivers of economic performance. In macroeconomic models, the role of the financial system was often reduced to the determination of a yield curve and stock prices, based mostly on the expectation hypothesis with fixed term premiums. Fluctuations were seen as regular random shocks. This does not fit the financial crisis, where the best metaphor is plate tectonics and earthquakes.

Financial crises are characterised by non-linearities and positive feedback whereby shocks are strongly amplified rather than damped as they propagate. And rather than returning to the status quo when the shock ends, financial crises are followed by long periods of depressed output. Another non-linearity comes from the interaction between public debt and the banking system, a mechanism known as "doom loops". This played a central role early in the euro crisis. Higher public debt leads to worries about public debt restructuring, decreasing the value of the bonds held by financial institutions, leading in turn to a decrease in their capital, worries about their health, and the expectation that the state may have to bail them out and be itself in trouble as a result.

In contrast to the standard pre-crisis view, non-linearities like this can amplify initial shocks, potentially leading to implosive paths, and strong policy challenges. We are in an environment of low nominal and real interest rates, and may be for the foreseeable future. An environment that forces a rethink not only of monetary, but also of fiscal and financial policies. So far, the focus has been primarily on monetary policy. The binding lower bound on short term nominal interest rates (zero, or slightly negative) limited the scope of monetary policy to sustain demand during the recovery. The limits of monetary policy imply a larger role for other policies, in particular fiscal policy. If the interest rate is below the growth rate, could this be a signal that the economy is dynamically inefficient, in which case larger public debt is actually not only feasible, but also desirable? If the economy is dynamically efficient, but the safe rate is below the growth rate, can the state still issue debt without ever paying it back? If it can, should it?

Low interest rates also have implications for financial regulation and macro prudential policy. It has been argued that a combination of human nature, leading to search for yield, and of agency issues, lead to more risk taking when interest rates are low. Also, by inflating asset values and reducing debt service costs, low rates may also lead to high leverage.

Given the limits to monetary policy, and neutral interest rates below growth rates, fiscal policy will inevitably play a much more active role in stabilisation. However, fiscal policy faces a highly unusual environment. Debt levels relative to GDP are high by historical standards, but interest rates on government debt are low, and in many countries, they are expected to remain lower than growth rates for some time to come. As a consequence, levels of government debt service relative to GDP are low by historical standards.

These evolutions raise two issues. The first is how fiscal policy can be used as a stabilisation tool. Another issue is the complexity of "multipliers", i.e. the effects of fiscal policy on demand and output, of their dependence on the specific type of fiscal adjustment and the economic environment.

Automatic stabilisers can be made more potent and effective with policy effort. And with the interest rate likely to remain below the growth rate for some time to come, the usual discussion of debt sustainability must be re-examined. At a minimum, debt consolidation can take place more slowly and there are additional arguments for debt-financed increased public investment.

Based on recent experience, a large fraction of instability in advanced economies over the next decades is likely to be associated with financial instability. This raises the issues of crisis prevention and crisis resolution. Some believe that policymakers need stronger tools for responding to financial strains, others that the moral hazard associated with the excessive availability of bailout funds was an important contributor to the excessive risk taking that led to the crisis. To a substantial extent, crises have their roots not in conscious risk taking by financial institutions, but in events that they do not anticipate, and so cannot be changed by altering incentives. Moreover, the provision of liquidity to combat runs may not represent a moral hazard cost because it need not be socially costly. The US government made a profit on the TARP programme of support for financial institutions.

For crisis prevention, the efficacy of capital regulation and stress tests, and the desirability of time varying regulatory policies to promote stability are central issues. However, claims that the system would weather a storm far worse than 2008 without any large institution needing to raise capital probably say more about stress test methodologies than they do about banking system robustness. A major policy error made in the 2008 crisis was the failure of regulatory authorities in the United States to force the raising of capital or at least the reduction of dividend payments and stock repurchases in the spring and summer of 2008, even as markets were seriously concerned about the health of the financial system.

While regulatory policies that are more responsive to changes in firms' economic capital are desirable, time-varying capital requirements or leverage limits may not be. It is difficult to identify bubbles or excessive credit booms ex ante and even more difficult to confidently identify them far enough ahead of their bursting to make countercyclical policy worthwhile. These considerations suggest financial stability benefits of higher and constant capital ratios, rather than lower and cyclically sensitive ones.

One of the most interesting findings of research since the crisis is that, leaving aside the risk that some activity shifts to the shadow banking sector (which thus needs to be regulated as well) higher capital ratios have limited effects on either the cost of funds for banks or on bank lending. Higher capital ratios than the current regulatory ratios may therefore be appropriate. For the best mix between financial regulation and macro prudential policy, having higher and constant capital ratios rather than lower and varying ones is likely to be more conducive to the maintenance of financial stability.

Sources

NAEC seminar "Rethinking macroeconomic policy", OECD, 5 July 2018
http://www.oecd.org/naec/events/rethinking-macroeconomic-policy.htm

"Rethinking Stabilization Policy. Back to the Future", Olivier Blanchard. Lawrence Summers, NBER Working Paper No. 24179, December 2017 http://www.nber.org/papers/w24179

26. The monetary system: master or servant?

Ann Pettifor

High levels of unemployment or under-employment, falling incomes, housing crises, and obscene levels of inequality have led to the rise of counter-movements in all the leading economies. Karl Polanyi foresaw this in the 1940s, in The Great Transformation: "No sooner will today's utopians have institutionalised their ideal of a global economy, apparently detached from political, social, and cultural relations, than powerful counter-movements—from the right no less than the left—would be mobilised". The current economic disorder that is helping to fuel populism is largely caused by the lack of transparency, and the intangibility of the international financial system. Widespread ignorance of the workings of the great public good that is our monetary system has made society vulnerable. If democracies are to make finance the servant to the real economy, the public must gain greater understanding of the monetary system.

Ignorance of the workings of the system is compounded by the fact that many economists chose to ignore it, until as Olivier Blanchard says, the crisis forced macroeconomists to (re)discover the role and the complexity of the financial sector, and the danger of financial crises. These economists chose to ignore reality because of the failings of the traditional approach to finance. In 1961 the newly-created OECD, encouraged by 'classical' economists proposed to turbocharge the economy. They championed an unsustainable and delusional new target for something they named "growth", 50 percent over the decade. They also pushed policies for financial liberalisation, although it would take several decades for these changes to be fully implemented. These policies led to a series of credit booms – regarded as 'infinite booms' by for example, traders in sub-prime mortgages and collateralised debt obligations. The situation was one of "all competition and no control", both as regards demand-side measures, such as limits on loans-to-value ratios, and supply-side actions, including lending and interest rate ceilings, reserve and capital requirements, and supervisory guidance. Policy and regulation require boundaries, but finance capital abhors boundaries. The result is an international monetary system run by the equivalent of the Sorcerer's Apprentice. In the absence of the Sorcerer – regulatory democracy – financial risk-takers and fraudsters have, since 1971, periodically crashed the global economy and ruined the lives of millions of people. There is no such thing as effective global regulation. Global financiers want to be free to use the magic of money creation to flood the global economy with 'easy' money, and just as frequently to starve economies of any affordable finance.

If we want to strengthen democracy, then we must subordinate bankers to their role as servants of the economy. Capital control over both inflows and outflows is a vital tool for doing so. In other words, if we really want to 'take back control' we will have to bring offshore capital back onshore. That is the only way to restore order to the domestic economy, but also to the global economy.

Monetary relationships must be carefully managed – by public, not private authority. Loans must primarily be deployed for productive employment and income-generating activity. Speculation leads to capital gains that can rise exponentially. But speculation can also lead to catastrophic losses. Loans for rent-seeking and speculation, gambling or betting, must be made inadmissible.

Money lent must not be burdened by high, unpayable real rates of interest. Rates of interest for short- and long-term, in real terms, safe and risky – must, again, be managed by public, not private authority if they are to be sustainable and repayable, and if debt is not to lead to systemic failure. Keynes explained how that could be done with his Liquidity Preference Theory according to which interest is the reward for giving up liquidity and rates are lower on short-term securities because investors are not sacrificing liquidity for as long as with other securities.

Both the domestic and international system are socially constructed, man-made systems. Just as they were built by society, so they can be transformed by society, as happened during the 'golden age' of economics from 1945 -71. The good news is that if well-managed, the social relationships that make up our monetary system are potentially infinite, unlike natural resources or human capital. A publicly-backed monetary system can provide for all of society's needs, including the very costly requirement to transform the economy away from fossil fuels. Under a sound monetary system, there need never be a shortage of finance.

The very real possibility of using public awareness, understanding, and political will to restore such a system is why I see a 'horizon of hope' for a world that appears to be heading towards another dark age.

Sources

NAEC workshop on financial markets, OECD, 20 October 2017, https://oecdtv.webtv-solution.com/4106/or/committee_on_financial_markets_naec_workshop.html

The Production of Money: How to Break the Power of Bankers, Ann Pettifor, Verso Books, 2017

"The Production of Money", LSE, 8 February, 2017
http://www.lse.ac.uk/Events/2017/02/20170208t1830vOT/The-Production-of-Money

27. Regulatory reform and equity

John Vickers

Regulatory reform of the financial system has gone in in the right direction. Structural reform got started in the United Kingdom by way of ring-fencing, which is a good thing to do, but it's not happening anywhere else, and that is disappointing. We need to go a lot further in terms of beefing up the equity capital in banks and other financial institutions. However, the official word globally and in the United Kingdom is that there is no need, where we've got to is just fine. It's a long way short of fine.

It's strange that people in the financial sector, in the banks themselves, and the regulatory community, with some exceptions, share a consensus that we've done very well, we've got to a good place. On the other hand, in the opinion of economists outside that group, again with some exceptions, we're not even halfway there. For such a big public policy question as how safe to make the banks, a question that is so important for how the market economy works, it is worrying to have these different expert groups such a long way apart. I feel that the economists have the best of this argument.

There is some very low cost, even free, insurance to be had by over time by gradually building up equity buffers, and then the odds of another severe crisis would be reduced. You can never say never, but if and when the next crisis hits, we'd be in a better place to withstand it. The question here is the proportion of shareholder-funded equity, how large a multiple of shareholder equity capital should the banks be allowed to grow to. Even after all the reform efforts, big banks, or the very biggest perhaps, can still go highly leveraged, but the academic view is that this is too much.

The issue is to decide what are the costs and benefits. Do we have a safer system, better incentives, better decision-making in place for when the next crisis hits? Are we better placed to absorb the losses, pay the costs? For society as a whole, it's not so clear what those costs are, provided you phase them in over a good length of time. One of the lessons of the crisis for economists is we need to think much more carefully about how the system is regulated and run, and it should be the main spirit of thinking about the financial system.

When I chaired the UK Independent Commission on Banking, we faced a dilemma on this issue. We felt that the baseline global regulation was not strong enough, but we were making recommendations just for the United Kingdom, and there's a limit to how far one country, even a sizeable one like the United Kingdom, can go above the global baseline. So our recommendation concerned British retail banks, and with retail there is less of a risk of all the banks migrating somewhere else. We wanted quite a significant chunk over and above the proposed global baseline, and at the same time, we would have said that the global baseline itself should have been much higher. But of course we didn't have a say in that decision.

When you line up the costs and benefits and do the analysis, I think the official view is left a bit stranded. The weight of evidence is that we have not gone far enough. Today, the economy generally is a better state than it was in the years immediately following the crisis, so there is an opportunity to go further and build it up. It could be done. There are political reasons why it's difficult, but there are no technical obstacles to doing it.

Now that we're ten years on from the financial crisis, people talk about the pendulum swinging back. It may be so when we should be pushing forward. I'm not saying, and I don't think anyone is saying, there's a bigger crisis just around the corner. I am saying though that we're in a reasonably calm situation at the moment, even if debt issues are building up in the world economy, so let's take this opportunity, let's build on the progress that has been made to go a number of steps further.

In the years immediately after the crisis, you had a firm line taken in the United Kingdom and with the then administration in the United States and in Switzerland. It's not entirely a coincidence that the Swiss had two enormous banks in relation to the size of the Swiss economy, just as we in the United Kingdom had some huge banks in relation to our economy. The too-big-to-fail issue is particularly prominent in economies like ours, but the banks say that where we've got to is just fine. They would point to the new resolution regimes that bail-in debt to say they can lower the estimate of how much equity capital is needed.

I think that's the wrong approach. I like the bail-in debt resolution regimes, where instead of the taxpayer bailing out the bank, the bank's creditors and shareholders recapitalise the bank by converting some of its debt into common shares. But I see bail-in as a complement, an add-on, not a reason to lower the equity capital requirements.

It would be awful if we had a repeat of the crisis, and in some ways, I think that we are even worse off, or could be even worse off, than last time. Monetary policy is at the limits, you can't do that again because we've already fired all the ammunition if you like. And the political consequences of the rise of populism in various places that we've seen have a lot to do with the financial crisis. If you had another problem in the financial system well within living memory, it could be calamitous, not just in economic terms but in society and politics more generally. The stakes are very high and it's important therefore that this issue gets more prominence; that we have the policy debate and let the best argument win. I think the evidence points to a need for more equity capital, but I'm not at the table with those who decide.

Source

NAEC Financial markets workshop, OECD, 20 October 2017,
https://oecdtv.webtv-solution.com/4106/or/committee_on_financial_markets_naec_workshop.html

John Vickers on reform of financial markets since the 2008 crisis https://youtu.be/JOXbbd_kHX4

28. Monetary finance

Adair Turner

"Monetary finance" means running a fiscal deficit (or a higher deficit than would otherwise be the case) which is not financed by the issue of interest-bearing debt, but by an increase in the monetary base. Milton Friedman described this as "helicopter money", with the government printing dollar bills and then using them to make a lump-sum payment to citizens. Today it could involve either a tax cut or a public expenditure increase which would not otherwise occur. It could be one-off or repeated. It would typically involve the creation of additional deposit rather than paper money, initially in the government's own current accounts, and then transferred into private deposit accounts either as a tax cut or through additional public expenditure. The money could be "created" in a number of ways, but the choice between them has no substantive economic consequences. In all cases the consolidated balance sheet of the government and central bank together is the same; the monetary base of irredeemable non-interest-bearing money is increased; and the government is thus able to cut taxes or increase expenditure without incurring any future liability to pay more interest, or to redeem the capital value of the money created.

Technically, and excluding the impact of political dynamics, money finance deficits can always stimulate aggregate nominal demand, and will always do so more certainly and more powerfully than either debt financed fiscal deficits or pure quantitative easing operations. The scale of the resulting stimulus to nominal demand can be managed, and adjusted over time through the use of available policy tools. If therefore there exist circumstances in which economies might face a deficiency of aggregate nominal demand, money financed fiscal deficits are, in technical terms, a feasible and at times optimal policy option. However, if monetary finance is accepted as legal and technically feasible, biases in the political system may create incentives for its excessive use. In democracies, electoral cycles create incentives for governments to reduce taxes or increase public expenditures in the run-up to the election, or to avoid necessary fiscal consolidation. If money financed deficits were an available option, they might appear a costless way out of this constraint. While non-democratic political systems might in principle be free of such incentives, in many cases they depend for their stability on clientele patronage systems which are most easily lubricated by money creation.

In response to these biases, and to the macroeconomic harm which excessive monetary finance has produced in many economies, modern economic policy has gravitated to the consensus that the only way to contain the dangers of monetary finance is to prohibit it entirely. The central issue therefore is political, whether we can design political economy rules, responsibilities and relationships which can allow us to obtain the technically possible benefits of money finance while constraining the dangers of excessive mis-use.

We could place the use of monetary finance within the constraints of central bank independence and of inflation targeting, and preserve the legally defined self-denying ordinance which prevents politicians from enjoying discretion to implement inflationary policies. It would not however be acceptable for the central bank to determine the precise allocation of the fiscal resources thereby created; this should be done by the government. The guiding principle should be that the specific measures implemented should be credibly one-off. Tax cuts and specific investment programmes might meet this criterion, but increases in ongoing entitlement programmes which are difficult to reduce later would not.

One counter argument is that the effectiveness of monetary finance might be offset by anticipation of an "inflation tax" that would depress demand so that monetary financed deficits might be no more stimulative than deficits financed by debt. However, a money financed deficit will always stimulate nominal demand, while a debt financed deficit might not do so in some circumstances, so that the stimulative impact of a money financed deficit is always greater than or equal to that of a debt financed one. This is the case both where the economy is already at full employment/full potential output and where an increase in nominal demand can therefore only produce an increase in inflation; and in the case with underemployment/below full potential output, where an increase in nominal demand could produce some increase in real output as well as an inflationary effect.

Another question relates to the private sector asset counterpart to a consolidated public sector non-interest-bearing liability. The impact of money financed deficits will only differ fundamentally from debt-financed deficits if the additional monetary base created is permanently non-interest-bearing. But who would willingly hold non-interest-bearing money? The answer is that while no household or company needs to hold non-interest-bearing money once market interest rates have returned to significantly positive levels, monetary finance is only fully effective if the commercial banks are required to hold non-interest-bearing reserves at the central bank. If instead the central bank paid interest on these reserves, the difference between money financed deficits and debt financed deficits would be very significantly reduced. But if the commercial banks are required to hold non-interest-bearing reserves, while companies and households earn interest on their deposits at commercial banks, this is equivalent to imposing a tax on commercial bank credit intermediation.

Although money finance should only be used in extreme circumstances and as a one-off exercise, it is possible that secular stagnation with negative real long-term interest rates would mean using money to finance part of a fiscal deficit year after year because this would better than other options such as running debt financed fiscal deficits, meaning that public debt levels as percent of GDP either rise continuously or stabilise at a high level only sustainable if interest rates remain very low for ever.

To conclude, there is a technical case for using monetary finance in some circumstances. But before using it, we should address the political issue of how to ensure it will only be used in appropriate circumstances and appropriately moderate quantities.

Sources

NAEC seminar "Between debt and the devil", OECD, 20 May 2016
http://www.oecd.org/naec/events/between-debt-and-the-devil.htm

"The Case for Monetary Finance", IMF, November 5–6, 2015
https://www.imf.org/external/np/res/seminars/2015/arc/pdf/adair.pdf

"Monetary Finance: Mechanics & Complications" INET, May, 2016
https://www.ineteconomics.org/perspectives/blog/monetary-finance-mechanics-complications

"Why a future tax on bank credit intermediation does not offset the stimulative effect of money financed deficits", INET, August 2016 https://www.ineteconomics.org/research/research-papers/why-a-future-tax-on-bank-credit-intermediation-does-not-offset-the-stimulative-effect-of-money-finance-deficits

29. What has changed since the crisis?

Willem Buiter

Few lessons have been learnt from the global financial crisis (GFC) and expressed in legal, regulatory and other institutional reforms, and some were the wrong lessons. We may know more about the observable drivers of financial crisis risk, but not enough to make it likely that we will see the next crisis coming. We still cannot confidently identify asset bubbles, so the bubbles that will precede the next financial crash will not have been identified by those in a position to act. On a global scale, the lack of progress in sorting out the distribution of capital requirements across a multinational financial institution is worrying. There is still "cognitive" regulatory capture whereby regulators internalise the objectives, interests and perception of reality of those they are meant to regulate and supervise in the public interest.

There have been attempts to address the perverse incentives through remuneration structures that involve deferred compensation, and banks are better capitalised now. That is good news, but banks still hold too little capital relative to their debt obligations and other sources of leverage, while systemically important non-bank financial intermediaries remain undercapitalised and have probably increased their share of total financial intermediation because of tighter regulation of banks. Banks can still hold their own domestic-currency-denominated sovereign debt with zero capital requirements and without any concentration or exposure limit. In the Eurozone, this strengthens the doom loop between barely solvent sovereigns and barely solvent banks.

In a number of countries, retail banking activities have been ring-fenced. It is difficult to see what problem this is the solution to. Lending to households and SMEs is also very risky, so there is no good case for separating the 'responsible' retail banking activities from the 'casino' activities of investment banks and other financial intermediaries. There is, however a need for macroprudential instruments to reduce the likelihood of financial and credit booms and bubbles, or the magnitude of the inevitable bust, to acceptable levels. Policy rates, the exchange rate and the size and composition of the central bank balance sheet are not sufficient. This requires countercyclical capital requirements; countercyclical liquidity requirements; countercyclical loan-to-value, loan-to-income or debt-service-to-income ratios; countercyclical margin requirements for equity etc. The cycle is the financial cycle, which may differ from the business cycle.

The operations of central banks should be rethought too. Many central banks have come out of the GFC with greatly enhanced supervisory and regulatory roles, but traditional central bank operational independence for monetary policy cannot be extended to these enhanced functions. The crisis reminded us that the primary responsibility of the central bank is financial stability. But central banks during the GFC created moral hazard and engaged in inappropriate quasi-fiscal activities by not heeding the third of Bagehot's guideposts for an effective lender of last resort (LLR): lend freely; lend against collateral that would be good during normal times and if held to maturity; and lend at a penalty rate. Moreover, the Dodd-Frank Act weakens the future ability of the Fed to act as LLR by restricting its ability to provide idiosyncratic support to financial institutions. In addition, the Federal Deposit Insurance Corporation can no longer issue blanket guarantees of bank debt as it did in October 2008, and the US Treasury will not be able to repeat its guarantee of money market funds, as it did in September 2008.

Today's debt burdens have not yet become un-financeable debt service burdens, but when neutral interest rates and credit risk spreads normalise, debt service burdens are likely to become unmanageable for many debtors. It is true that, for domestic-currency-denominated, nominal debt, a shift from the private sector to the public sector reduces the risk of default. There are however political and economic constraints on the ability of the sovereign to raise taxes (and to cut public spending) to cover these debts. In the Eurozone moreover, governments do not have the ultimate control of monetary issuance by their national central banks unless they are willing to leave the monetary union.

As well as the need for an LLR, the crisis reminded us of the need for a market maker of last resort (MMLR) given the significant amount of financial intermediation through the financial and capital markets. The LLR provides funding liquidity and the MMLR provides market liquidity. The GFC likewise made clear the need for a global LLR/MMLR. The IMF does not have the resources to do this and the greatest achievement of the Fed during the GFC was that it became the de facto global LLR, through the use of the liquidity swap lines (reciprocal currency arrangements). This prevented a complete financial collapse in Europe, but it is unfortunate that no swap lines were made available to the central banks of the "fragile five" (Brazil, India, Indonesia, South Africa and Turkey).

Conventional monetary policy space is likely to be very limited (especially outside the United States) when the next financial crisis and recession hit. Lack of fiscal space will likely restrict the scope for public spending increases and/or tax cuts if the resulting fiscal deficits cannot be monetised. The lack of fiscal space will become acute when neutral interest rates and credit risk spreads normalise. Helicopter money drops are the only effective way to stimulate demand when the economy is in a liquidity trap and there is limited fiscal space for debt-financed fiscal stimuli. We are not well positioned to deliver here.

Limited and selective learning has taken place by policy makers and by monetary, supervisory and regulators. Some of the lessons drawn have lowered the ability of the central bank to act effectively as LLR/MMLR. The banking sector may be slightly more resilient. It is not enough, however, to prevent another major financial crisis or even to postpone it by much. Nor is it enough to mitigate the impact on the real economy.

Source

"10 Years after the failure of Lehman Brothers: What have we learned?" NAEC Conference, OECD, 13-14 September 2018, http://www.oecd.org/naec/10-years-after-the-crisis/

30. Bad policies encourage and tolerate excessive fragility

Anat Admati

Developed economies rely on chains of commitments between individuals and businesses of all sizes to enable consumption and investments and to share risks. Intermediaries such as banks and institutional investors are often important participants in these chains, making loans to individuals and businesses, investing their own and other people's money in the financial claims of large corporations. Financial firms also create and facilitate trade in asset-backed securities representing claims on baskets of assets, and in derivative securities whose payoffs depend on the realisation of certain events.

Central banks and governments play a critical role in the financial system. Government bonds trade alongside other securities in financial markets. Central banks lend to financial institutions, and increasingly participate directly in the markets by buying or accepting as collateral not only government bonds but also mortgage securities and corporate bonds. By setting the terms of the loans they make and determining which assets to purchase and at what quantities, central banks and governments impact the allocation and pricing of financial claims, effectively choosing winners and losers. How others in the economy are affected by government and central bank actions can depend critically on decisions made by financial intermediaries and other corporations, for example whether they use funds to make payouts to shareholders or invest in employees' welfare or otherwise.

Excessive borrowing by households and financial institutions, combined with ineffective regulations, were key causes of the 2007-2009 financial crisis. Many troubled banks received massive support from governments and central banks during and since the crisis, and they benefitted from the rescue of others (such as the insurance company AIG or the Greek government). The lingering weakness of banks and households lengthened the post-crisis recession.

Many claim that reforms have made the financial system much safer, but in fact the system has not changed substantially in the last decade, and it remains too fragile, opaque and distorted. Policymakers failed to learn the lessons of the financial crisis and the new rules are complex, poorly designed and inadequate, exposing the public to unnecessary risk. Perhaps the most glaring regulatory failure in the run-up to the financial crisis in 2008 and through the last decade that included highly profitable years for the banking sector, was allowing them to deplete their ability to absorb losses by making payouts to shareholders (in the form of dividends and share buybacks) rather than retain these and reinvest these profits on behalf of their shareholders and to be better prepared for economic shocks. Cash paid out to shareholders is no longer available to repay depositors and other creditors. When governments and central banks rescue banks, the shareholders and managers who had benefitted from the prior gains effectively pass on some of the losses to innocent taxpayers.

The distorted incentives of heavily indebted corporations are not unique to banking. Making payouts to shareholders, continuing to borrow, and selling assets (or laying off employees) instead of retaining profits and raising new equity can benefit managers and shareholders by shifting costs, risks and losses to others. A "leverage ratchet" dynamics makes corporate borrowing addictive and inefficient. This problem is particularly relevant for banks, whose love of borrowing is due to their naturally high level of indebtedness (in the process of taking deposits) and is further enabled and encouraged by explicit and implicit guarantees. Unless regulators intervene, and with supports from central banks, dysfunctional "zombie" banks may persist for extended periods of time, hiding their weaknesses and gambling for resurrection.

Corporate tax codes in most jurisdictions, which subsidise debt relative to equity, are among the key reasons corporations borrow excessively. These tax subsidies have no good rationale or justification. They are as perverse as subsidising a polluting technology when clean and otherwise equally costly alternatives are available. The persistence of bad and harmful policies is no excuse for allowing it to continue. Abolishing distortive debt subsidies is long overdue.

We find counterproductive debt subsidies in other parts of the economy. For example, some nations, such as the United States and the Netherlands, provide tax and other subsidies to mortgage debt, which encourages excessive borrowing to invest in real estate and distorts household decisions and housing markets. If home ownership is worthy of public subsidies, governments can find ways to subsidise equity rather than debt funding of homes. Similarly, the student debt crisis in the United States reflects counterproductive policies in the name of supporting higher education. The policy creates heavy and harsh debt burdens, subsidises for-profit colleges, including those providing sub-par education, and raises the cost of higher education.

When borrowers default or become insolvent, they may file for bankruptcy. The legal processes that ensue vary in different jurisdictions and for different borrowers, and they can be complicated, lengthy and costly. Cross-border resolution of large multinational financial institutions is virtually intractable, a problem that has been known for decades yet remains largely unsolved. Worse, some bankruptcy provisions, such as broad "safe haven" exemptions to derivatives and repo (sale and repurchase) agreements favour some creditors, mostly from within the financial system, over others, and ultimately encourage fragility. Finally, distortions in the setting and implementation of accounting rules, auditing, and credit ratings further increase the opacity of the financial system.

Fuelled by persistently low interest rates and by yield-chasing investors willing to overlook risks, corporations have binged on debt in recent years, planting the seeds of a debt crisis before the onslaught of Covid-19. The disruptions caused by the pandemic led numerous affected individuals and businesses to financial distress and the inability to fulfil all the promises they had made. Governments and central banks stepped in to prevent some defaults or delay harsh consequences, for example by mandating temporary freezes on foreclosures and evictions, providing unemployment benefits, cash grants, and loans. Central banks have poured trillions into financial institutions and asset purchase programmes.

These actions have propped up financial markets, but also created distortions and added to the high mountain of debt, which will have to be dealt with at some point. Similar to the financial crisis of 2007-2009, the extraordinary interventions favour investors and corporations and do not reach many parts of the economy that are most in need, creating disconnect between financial markets and the rest of the economy and exacerbating income and wealth inequality. Despite the risk of massive losses from the slowdown of the economy, many banks are still allowed to make payouts to shareholders and harm the public.

Recklessness in finance goes beyond excessive borrowing and includes many cases of fraud, money laundering and other law evasion, only some of which are periodically revealed. Large fines, with no major consequences for individuals who could have done more to prevent wrongdoings, fail to prevent repeated scandals. We must re-examine the workings of our justice systems in a corporate context.

In some parts of our lives, such as aviation safety, complex systems operate remarkably safely, including across national borders. In the financial sector, however, recklessness persists because of political economy forces and the benefit that many who collectively control the system derive from its fragility. Covid-19 might serve as a wake-up call.

Sources

The Bankers' New Clothes: What's Wrong with Banking and What to Do about It (with Martin Hellwig), Princeton University Press, March 2013 http://bankersnewclothes.com/

"The Leverage Ratchet Effect" (with Peter DeMarzo, Martin Hellwig and Paul Pfleiderer), *Journal of Finance*, 2018, 145-198. https://admati.people.stanford.edu/publications/leverage-ratchet-effect

"The Parade of Bankers' New Clothes Continues: 34 Flawed Claims Debunked" (with Martin Hellwig), revised August, 2019. https://admati.people.stanford.edu/publications/parade-bankers-new-clothes-continues-34-flawed-claims-debunked

"The Missed Opportunity and Challenge of Capital Regulation", *National Institute Economic Review*, February 2016, 235: R4-14. https://admati.people.stanford.edu/publications/missed-opportunity-and-challenge-capital-regulation

"It Takes a Village to Maintain a Dangerous Financial System", *Just Financial Markets? Finance in a Just Society*, Lisa Herzog, editor, Oxford University Press, 2017. https://admati.people.stanford.edu/publications/it-takes-village-maintain-dangerous-financial-system

31. Public debt and the new (old) normal

Michael Jacobs

The coronavirus crisis has raised government deficits and debt to levels not seen since the Second World War. As they closed their economies down to control the public health risk, governments in all developed countries have been forced into unprecedented increases in spending. Resources have been poured into health systems; radical measures taken to keep companies afloat and workers in jobs; welfare payments have spiralled as unemployment has risen. At the same time the closedown of economic activity has caused tax revenues to collapse.

The OECD's *Economic Outlook* in June 2020 reported that in the first three months of the crisis public debt-to-GDP ratios rose by 10% or more in almost all OECD countries. The report forecasts debt-to-GDP levels in 2021 of over 100% in the United States, United Kingdom and the Euro area as a whole, with Japan's reaching around 250%. These ratios reflect not just much higher budget deficits, but lower GDP.

For many years, the orthodox economic view has been that deficits and debt levels of these kinds are extremely damaging to medium-term growth, and so to be avoided at almost all costs. Following the 2008 financial crisis, this view led to the implementation across Europe of severe austerity policies, including the socially devastating measures imposed on its peripheral members by the Eurozone.

This view had two main origins. Theoretically, it followed from the 'crowding out' thesis, which argued that high government borrowing required high interest rates to fund it in the short term and higher taxes in the long, both of which would deter private sector investment and spending. Empirically, it was bolstered by a famous 2010 paper by Reinhart and Rogoff, which claimed a consistent historical and cross-country pattern that debt-to-GDP ratios over 90% were associated with significantly lower growth rates.

The empirical basis of this paper was subsequently discredited, and the crowding out thesis had long been challenged by the Keynesian observation that in a recession there is insufficient private sector investment to be deterred, and public borrowing is the only way to sustain aggregate demand. But intellectual and policy inertia is powerful, and some version of the orthodox view persists in many commentaries about the current crisis. The question is being asked: how will we pay for all this extra public spending? Will we need a return to austerity to bring deficit and debt levels down to affordable levels?

There is now wide consensus among macroeconomists that the answer to this is no. This is for four crucial reasons.

First, since public borrowing is always partly a question of intergenerational equity (with current spending paid for out of future income), the severity of current economic conditions makes a critical difference to the calculus. We are now entering the most severe global recession at least since the 1930s, and in many countries perhaps for centuries. By the end of 2020 the OECD forecasts unemployment at over 10% on average across the OECD and the Euro area, with higher rates if second outbreaks of the coronavirus occur. In these circumstances current public spending will not be enough – new stimulus packages will be required to create jobs through public works and training schemes, infrastructure investment, subsidies to key sectors and probably tax cuts. If this is not done the long-term 'scarring' effects of business failures and unemployment will be even more severe than already being experienced. The idea that such measures should *not* be implemented in order to save future generations from higher debt levels is patently absurd. 'Future generations' are today's young people, who will suffer most from high and lasting unemployment. The cost-benefit calculus is clearly on the side of even higher deficits now.

This is particularly true, second, because in these deep recessionary conditions it is only through public spending that growth will resume, and it is only through growth that debt levels will eventually fall. Household spending, corporate investment and global trade are projected to pick up only slowly and uncertainly over the next few years, and in these circumstances only government spending can fill the gap in aggregate demand. As the experience of austerity after 2010 demonstrated, too early a withdrawal of government spending leads to slower growth, and therefore to more slowly-falling debt. Austerity in recession is self-defeating.

Third, the level of interest rates at which many governments can currently borrow makes the cost-benefit calculus completely different from previous periods. What matters to future generations is not the ratio of debt to GDP itself, but the cost of servicing that debt. At low interest rates – in some countries governments can now borrow at negative real rates for 20 years ahead – the cost of servicing debt is extremely low. This means that the return on investment required to justify current expenditure is much lower than in the past. As long as the nominal interest rate is below the nominal growth rate of the economy, debt to GDP will gradually stabilise and then decline (provided the government's primary budget balance remains stable). These are not the conditions in which the previous orthodoxy was developed, when interest rates were assumed to exceed GDP growth rates, and almost always did.

Fourth, central banks are now much more involved in buying government debt than in the past. The expansion of quantitative easing (QE) during this crisis has seen central banks buy up large quantities of government debt, and their continuing willingness to do so is an important reason that interest rates are projected to stay low. The prevailing assumption behind QE since the financial crisis has been that at some point in the future central banks will sell the debt back into the market, but almost no such 'unwinding' had occurred before the current crisis struck, and the new wave of asset purchases has made the prospect recede even further. But it doesn't matter. Central banks can hold government debt indefinitely, if necessary. So long as today's low inflationary expectations persist, there is no reason why they should not do so.

So there is no need for a return to austerity, or for governments to seek to pay back their newly-raised debts in a short period of time. We shall simply have to get used to sustained high debt-to-GDP ratios, in some cases over 100%, and to accept that they are worth the cost. This will be the new macroeconomic normal.

Or more accurately, it will be a return to an old normal. After the Second World War, national debt was even higher than today. In the United States it peaked at 113% of GDP in 1945, in the United Kingdom 250%. These levels were reached because governments in both countries took it for granted that winning the war was more important than the cost of future debt. So instead of a return to austerity after the war, the immediate post-war period saw an expansion of public expenditure on health, housing and welfare services. These contributed to growth, as well as to a reduction in inequalities (which also contributed to growth), and there was almost no demand for the debt to be repaid quickly. It took 15 years for US public debt to return to its pre-war level, and thirty years for UK public debt to return to 50% of GDP (in 1975). In both countries in this period the central bank bought up significant portions of the debt and kept it on its own balance sheet.

After the financial crash a popular economic metaphor was that the national economy is like a household. It must live within its means, and pay back its debts. But the metaphor was wrong then, and it is even less applicable today. Today the appropriate metaphor is that the coronavirus crisis is like a war. During times of war, governments spend what it takes to defeat the enemy, and borrow from their central banks to do so. They then pay the debt back over a long period, relying on investment and growth (and some inflation). Today we must do the same. For it is not just a war against the coronavirus that we face today. We also face a climate and environmental emergency. This demands much higher levels of investment in low-carbon infrastructure, industrial transformation and nature restoration. As governments contemplate the new phase of the current crisis, they have a huge opportunity to tackle mass unemployment and recession through spending on green recovery measures. Anxiety about the levels of government debt that will result should not prevent them.

32. Coronavirus crisis lays bare the risks of financial leverage, again

Martin Wolf
© The Financial Times, 28 April 2020

This time it is capital markets, rather than banks, that have to reform.

The scale of the financial disarray reflects in part the size of the economic shock. It is also a reminder of what the late Hyman Minsky taught us: debt causes fragility. Since the global financial crisis, indebtedness has continued to rise. In particular, the indebtedness of non-financial companies rose by 13 percentage points between September 2008 and December 2019, relative to global output. The indebtedness of governments, which assumed much of the post-financial crisis burden, rose by 30 percentage points. This shift on to the shoulders of governments will now happen again, on a huge scale.

IMF's April 2020 *Global Financial Stability Report* gives a clear overview of the fragilities. Significant risks arise from asset managers as forced sellers of assets, leveraged parts of the nonfinancial corporate sector, some emerging countries, and even some banks. While the latter are not the centre of this story, reasons for concern remain, despite past strengthening. This shock, the report states, is likely to be even more severe than envisaged in the IMF's stress tests. Banks remain highly leveraged institutions, especially if we use market valuations of assets. As the report notes: "Median market-adjusted capitalisation is now higher than in 2008 only in the US." The chances that banks will need more capital is not small.

Yet it is capital markets that lie at the heart of this saga. Specific stories are revealing. The Bank for International Settlements has studied one weird episode in mid-March when markets for benchmark government bonds experienced extraordinary turbulence. This happened because of the forced selling of Treasury securities by investors seeking "to exploit small yield differences through the use of leverage". This is the type of "long-short strategy" made infamous by the failure of Long-Term Capital Management in 1998. It is also a strategy vulnerable to rising volatility and declining market liquidity. These cause mark-to-market losses. Then, as margin is called in, investors are forced to sell assets to redeem loans.

Another story elucidated by the BIS tells of emerging economies. An important recent development has been the rising use of local currency bonds to finance government spending. But when the prices of these bonds fell in the crisis, so did exchange rates, increasing the losses borne by foreign investors. These exchange-rate collapses worsen the solvency of domestic borrowers (notably businesses) with debts denominated in foreign currency. The inability to borrow in domestic currency used to be called "original sin". This has not gone, argue the BIS's Augustin Carstens and Hyun Song Shin. It has just "shifted from borrowers to lenders".

Yet another significant capital-market issue is the role of private equity and other high-leverage strategies in increasing expected returns, but also the risks, in corporate finance. Such approaches are almost perfectly designed to reduce resilience in periods of economic and financial stress. Governments and central banks have now been forced to bail them out, just as they were forced to bail out banks in the financial crisis. This will reinforce "heads, I win; tails, you lose" strategies. So vast is the size of central bank and government rescues that moral hazard must be pervasive.

The crisis has revealed much fragility. It has also demonstrated yet again the uncomfortably symbiotic relationship between the financial sector and the state. In the short run, we must try to get through this crisis with as little damage as possible. But we must also learn from it for the future.

A systematic evaluation of the frailties of capital markets, comparable to what was done with banks after the financial crisis, is now essential. One issue is how emerging economies reduce the impact of the new version of "original sin". Another is what to do about private sector leverage and the way in which risk ends up on governments' balance sheets. I think of this as trying to run capitalism with the least possible risk-bearing capital. It makes little sense. This creates a microeconomic task - eliminating incentives for the private sector to fund itself so heavily via debt; and a macroeconomic one - reducing reliance on debt to generate aggregate demand.

The big question now is whether the essential systems that keep our societies running are adequately resilient. The answer is no. This is the sort of question the OECD's New Approaches to Economic Challenges Unit has dared to address. Inevitably, it has created much controversy. Yet it is admirable that an international organisation is daring to do so at all. The crisis has shown us why. We cannot afford complacency. We need to reassess the resilience of our economic, social and health arrangements. A focus on finance must be an important part of this effort.

33. The vulnerability of financial markets

Mathilde Mesnard and *Robert Patalano*

The global financial system remains inherently fragile and vulnerable to endogeneous evolutions as well as to shocks aring from within the financial system itself, as in 2008, or from outside, as with the Covid-19-triggered crisis. In such a complex adaptive system as the financial system, there are tipping points that create radical and sudden changes in behaviours, leading to instability or crisis, that will in turn be amplified due to negative spillovers and feedback loops between institutions and markets, and within and across borders that extend beyond national regulatory perimeters. Despite collective efforts by many OECD countries to implement a comprehensive suite of G20 financial reforms, Covid has illustrated new faultlines that have arisen in part due to unintended consequences, from concentrations to regulatory arbitrage and market fragmentation.

Sources of current financial vulnerability include the rise of global corporate debt in both advanced and emerging market economies, resulting from low interest rates and abundant liquidity. High levels of leverage increase firms' vulnerability to shocks, the more so in a low growth environment. Moreover, the current stock of outstanding corporate bonds has lower overall credit quality, higher payback requirements, longer maturities and inferior covenant protection. These characteristics could amplify the negative effects of any downturn on the non-financial sector and the overall economy.

A particular concern is linked to the rebound in the issuance of leveraged loans and collateralised loan obligations, now well over USD 2 trillion globally, and largely issued without financial covenants that typically protect leveraged lenders from excessive losses. Furthermore, a significant amount of speculative bonds and leveraged loans are held in open-ended investment funds. Unexpected sharp redemptions of funds in levels beyond liquidity buffers of such funds cause portfolio managers to sell these less-liquid assets to raise cash, and such forced asset sales propagate stress to other debt investors. The combination of corporate leverage and liquidity transformation of funds adds to systemic fragility during periods of stress.

Another potential source of crisis is the level of sovereign debt. Given the surge in sovereign borrowing needs in response to the pandemic, redemptions will increase substantially, exposing issuers to refinancing risks in the future. Moreover, despite efforts to strengthen banking systems, bank equity valuations have fallen to historically low levels amid the Covid crisis, as weak banking sector performance and weak asset quality in many countries considerably deteriorated in 2020.

In the longer term, there are also implications of climate change for market resilience and financial stability, with both physical risks related to the actual or expected economic costs of a continuation in climate change, and transition risks related to an adjustment towards a low-carbon economy. The manifestation of physical risks could lead to large losses, particularly in industries where exposure to fires, floods, and storms is more detrimental to performance. Growing physical risks will likely have an increasingly large impact on the stability of the financial system, unless countermeasures – both environmental and financial – are taken. A disorderly transition to a low carbon economy, for example in the form of an abrupt change in public policy not anticipated by market participants, could result in a sharp fall in asset prices as so-called stranded assets associated with fossil fuels are devalued, which could destabilise the financial system.

Improving market resilience and policy certainty is vital to help mitigate the unexpected and anticipated impacts from physical and transition risks, and financial markets are already moving in this direction. Sustainable finance, through environmental, social and governance (ESG) investing and green markets, is providing a wealth of information that can help market participants and regulators better assess the potential climate risks and take mitigating actions. Amid this progress, the current state of sustainable finance related to ESG and green finance is such that much greater transparency, consistency, and comparability of metrics and methodologies are needed to ensure that investors, from central banks to retail funds, have reliable market tools to help reduce fossil fuels and pivot toward renewable investments to facilitate an effective transition to low-carbon economies.

Physical and transition risks might combine, amplifying their overall effect on financial stability, with concentrated exposures in certain financial institutions. Climate-related risks may thus affect financial system resilience and give rise to abrupt increases in risk premia across a wide range of assets. The breadth and magnitude of climate-related risks might make these changes more pernicious than in the case of other economic risks. Moreover, the interaction of climate-related risks with other macroeconomic vulnerabilities could increase risks to financial stability. Therefore, it is critical that more in-depth steps are taken by financial authorities, related to stress testing of portfolios, more climate-friendly reserve managerment portfolios, and even consideration of greening of the financial system through collateral and monetary policy frameworks within existing central bank mandates.

In summary, as the NAEC Initiative has highlighted, there are currently many endogeneous sources of vulnerabilities within the global financial markets, as well as many already materialised or highly probable external shocks. Governments have made significant and globally coordinated efforts to address the consequences of the Covid crisis, in addition to efforts over the past decade to improve the resilience of the global financial system. Yet, this economic shock has illustrated that additional policy measures, based on new ways of considering systemic risks – be they pandemics or climate change – are urgently needed to ensure a resilient financial system that can set the foundation for sustainable and inclusive economic growth. We need to think the unthinkable when it comes to policy measures to deal with catastrophic tail risks, as Covid has demonstrated.

Sources

Boffo, R., C. Marshall and R. Patalano (2020), "ESG: The Environmental Pillar" *forthcoming*.

NGFS (2019), "A call for action: Climate change as a source of financial risk."

Patalano, R. and C. Roulet (2020), "Structural developments in global financial intermediation: The rise of debt and non-bank credit intermediation", *OECD Working Papers on Finance, Insurance and Private Pensions*, No. 44, OECD Publishing, Paris, https://doi.org/10.1787/daa87f13-en.

Roulet, C (2020), "Covid-19: Stress simulations of corporate debt." *forthcoming*

Roulet C. and Patalano, R (2020), "Covid-19: Non-performing loan losses and bank asset disposal strategies" *forthcoming*.

OECD (2019), Business and Finance Outlook: Trust in Business, Chapter 1.

OECD (2020), Business and Finance Outlook: Sustainable and Resilient Finance, *forthcoming*.

34. Do economists think between crises?

Alan Kirman

Economists have argued for two centuries now that if people are left to their own devices, the invisible hand will lead to a socially satisfactory state. Rough periods will occur of course, so one should just take appropriate measures to "get things back to normal". This faith is not justified by history. We have navigated from crisis to crisis, and leaving individuals and firms to their own devices does not produce the nirvana that many claim. The world has organised itself in a way that puts a high premium on short-run "efficiency" and "just in time" supply chains. The idea that one might want to have reserve capacities "just in case" has been dismissed and we are now paying heavily for that.

There is nothing unprecedented about today's crisis, notwithstanding claims that this is an entirely new situation for which we could not have been prepared. And that despite high profile figures such as Bill Gates arguing in a 2015 TED talk entitled "The Next Outbreak: We are not Ready" that we should not simply react to each crisis as it occurred but should be "playing epidemic and crisis games" the way the military play war games.

The structure of our system is conducive to its fragility, with short-term individualistic incentives within a framework that is increasingly interconnected and interdependent. As Andy Haldane's prophetic comparison in 2009 put it:

> *"Seizures in the electricity grid, degradation of ecosystems, the spread of epidemics and the disintegration of the financial system – each is essentially a different branch of the same network family tree".*

Ben Bernanke argued that:

> *"The best approach for dealing with this uncertainty is to make sure that the system is fundamentally resilient and that we have as many fail-safes and back-up arrangements as possible."*

Such observations soon faded from memory, and when the pandemic hit, few reactions from governments questioned the existing economic framework. President Emmanuel Macron was an exception:

> *"This pandemic reveals that there are goods and services that must be placed outside the laws of the market."*

This admission by someone regarded as a disciple of universal deregulation suggests that the "neo-liberal consensus" is being questioned, though impacts on economic policy remain to be seen.

The question is are we prepared to accept that our system will evolve through reactions to successive crises, or is it possible to analyse the nature of crises, to avoid having simply to react to each in turn? Although we have not created Bill Gates' powerful army of experts, many people thought deeply about major systemic disruptions. The OECD, for example, created the New Approaches to Economic Challenges (NAEC) initiative in 2012 to draw lessons from the 2008 crisis. NAEC emphasises the need to look at the world as a complex adaptive system whose behaviour is governed by the interaction between its components.

Economists now recognise the need to integrate the financial sector more effectively into macroeconomic policy thinking and NAEC contributors from fields as diverse as statistical physics and central banking have made proposals on how to do this. Contrary to conventional wisdom, becoming more connected has not made the financial network more robust. Macro characteristics such as robustness, radical uncertainty, or emergence cannot be deduced from even a detailed knowledge of the individual components. These characteristics call for simulations and computational models rather than analytical models which provide exact "solutions".

NAEC also focuses on another system characteristic, resilience, with Igor Linkov from the U.S. Corps of Army Engineers, as part of its mission to protect populations from major disasters. Linkov's work highlights the trade-offs between resilience and efficiency that the Covid-19 crisis has highlighted. Cutting hospital beds or relying on one supplier of protective equipment may have made health systems "more efficient", but we now see the price to be paid. Resilience is now one of the most frequently used words when the current pandemic is being discussed, yet had we taken it seriously the effects of the pandemic would have been much less severe.

Thinking systemically suggests that modern crises can soon lose their identities, with a health crisis becoming an economic crisis. The same is true for epidemics. Nobel Prize winner Angus Deaton explained the epidemic of "Deaths of Despair" from opioid addiction, alcoholism and stagnating wages as in fact the product of several epidemics each intimately related to the others (see Chapter 17). Likewise, Joshua Epstein, professor of epidemiology at NYU, views the current pandemic as a product of two epidemics, the disease itself and fear of the disease. One could add a third epidemic, as financial markets participants who were neither infected nor fearful are impacted by the first two epidemics through changes in stock market indices.

This highlights the importance of narratives. Nobel Laureate Bob Shiller emphasises that stories do not just explain economic policy, but also shape it. In the social media age, many narratives are based on widely shared fake news, but we should not confuse rapidity of diffusion with depth of impact. Analysis by David Chavalarias at the Paris Complexity Institute of millions of tweets and retweets during the French presidential campaign shows that fake news reinforces existing prejudices but does not convert those who are not sympathetic to it to begin with. Today, "getting back to normal" would resonate with those sympathetic to the narrative that has dominated economic policymaking over the last decades. These forces of inertia and vested interests resistant to change will quickly forget that the system cannot simply be put back on the rails and left to run as before, leaving us even worse prepared for the next disaster than for this one.

The encouraging return in the current crisis of expert opinion, notably from epidemiologists', highlights how economists have been paid little attention, despite the economic consequences of the pandemic. But if economists react to each crisis by immediately forecasting outcomes, their poor accuracy in the past may lead to them being ignored (or may cause misinformed panic). Much better to admit that with so much radical uncertainty, as John Kay and Mervyn King point out in their new book entitled Radical Uncertainty, "we simply don't know".

Sources

Rethinking the Financial Network, speech given by Andrew G Haldane, Chief Economist, Bank of England, at the Financial Student Association, Amsterdam, 28 April 2009
https://www.bankofengland.co.uk/speech/2009/rethinking-the-financial-network

Is Ben Bernanke Having Fun Yet? Profile of Ben Bernanke by Sewell Chan, *New York Times*,
May 15, 2010 https://archive.nytimes.com/www.nytimes.com/2010/05/16/business/16ben.html

National televised speech on Covid-19 by President Emmanuel Macron, 12 March 2020

Agent Zero and Integrative Economics, presentation by Joshua M. Epstein, Professor of Epidemiology, New York University School of Global Public Health, at the NAEC conference on Integrative Economics, OECD, 5 March 2020 https://www.oecd.org/naec/integrative-economics/

NAEC seminar "Narrative economics", Robert J. Shiller, OECD, 10 September 2019
http://www.oecd.org/naec/events/narrative-economics.htm

NAEC seminar "How Twitter is changing politics" David Chavalarias, Director of The Institute of Complex Systems, OECD, 22 November 2017,
https://oecdtv.webtv-solution.com/4047/or/general_secretariat_naec_seminar_on_social_media.html

www.ingramcontent.com/pod-product-compliance
Lightning Source LLC
Chambersburg PA
CBHW082109210326
41599CB00033B/6644